Using Microsoft® Windows® 8.1

Using Microsoft® Windows® 8.1

Part Number: 091128
Course Edition: 2.0

Acknowledgements

PROJECT TEAM

Author	Media Designer	Content Editor
Gail Sandler Jason Nufryk	Alex Tong	Tricia Murphy

Notices

Using Microsoft® Windows® 8.1

Lesson 1: Getting to Know PCs and the Windows 8.1 User Interface.. 1

Topic A: Identify Components of a Personal Computer.................. 2

Topic B: Sign In to Windows 8.1...7

Topic C: Navigate the Start Screen... 13

Lesson 2: Using Windows Store Apps and Navigation Features...23

Topic A: Access and Identify the Charms..................................... 24

Topic B: Windows Store Apps and Common Navigation Features...29

Topic C: Multitask with Apps... 34

Lesson 3: Working with Desktop Applications.............. 43

Topic A: Navigate the Desktop... 44

Topic B: Manage Files and Folders with File Explorer.................... 51

Topic C: Elements of a Desktop Window....................................... 60

Topic D: Create and Modify Files with Desktop Applications......... 68

Lesson 4: Using Internet Explorer 11........................... 79

Topic A: Navigate Internet Explorer 11....................................... 80

Topic B: Browse the Web... 87

Topic C: Use Internet Explorer 11 on the Desktop.................................. 99

Lesson 5: Customizing the Windows 8.1 Environment.........109

Topic A: Customize the Start Screen.. 110

Topic B: Customize the Desktop... 121

Lesson 6: Using Windows 8.1 Security Features.................. 129

Topic A: Set Privacy Levels and Passwords... 130

Topic B: Use Windows Defender..139

Topic C: Store and Share Files with OneDrive..143

Appendix A: Other Windows 8.1 Features............................ 153

Topic A: Create a New User Account...154

Topic B: File History...155

Appendix B: Help+Tips App..159

Appendix C: Windows 8.1 Navigation Summary..................................... 161

Lesson Labs... 169

Solutions... 175

Glossary.. 177

Index... 181

About This Course

Welcome to *Using Microsoft® Windows® 8.1*. Whether you're new to computers or have used them in the past, this class will help you become more comfortable using a personal computer (PC) and, more specifically, the Windows 8.1 interface. This course will help you to define what a PC is, and familiarize you with the Windows 8.1 user interface and its basic capabilities. In this course, you will explore Windows 8.1 and learn how to create documents, send email, browse the Internet, and share information between applications and with other users.

Course Description

Target Student

This course is designed for any end user, especially an individual new to computing, who needs to use the features and functionality of the Windows 8.1 operating system for personal and/or professional reasons.

Course Prerequisites

This course is intended for new computer users who want to use the basic tools and features of Windows 8.1. No particular prerequisite skills are required, but any previous exposure to personal computers and the Internet is helpful.

Course Objectives

Upon successful completion of this course, you will be able to perform basic work-related tasks on a PC running the Windows 8.1 operating system.

You will:

- Get to know PCs and the Windows 8.1 user interface.
- Use Windows Store apps and navigation features.
- Work with Desktop applications.
- Use Internet Explorer 11.
- Customize the Windows 8.1 environment.
- Use Windows 8.1 security features.

The LogicalCHOICE Home Screen

The LogicalCHOICE Home screen is your entry point to the LogicalCHOICE learning experience, of which this course manual is only one part. Visit the LogicalCHOICE Course screen both during and after class to make use of the world of support and instructional resources that make up the LogicalCHOICE experience.

Log-on and access information for your LogicalCHOICE environment will be provided with your class experience. On the LogicalCHOICE Home screen, you can access the LogicalCHOICE Course screens for your specific courses.

Each LogicalCHOICE Course screen will give you access to the following resources:

- eBook: an interactive electronic version of the printed book for your course.
- LearnTOs: brief animated components that enhance and extend the classroom learning experience.

Depending on the nature of your course and the choices of your learning provider, the LogicalCHOICE Course screen may also include access to elements such as:

- The interactive eBook.
- Social media resources that enable you to collaborate with others in the learning community using professional communications sites such as LinkedIn or microblogging tools such as Twitter.
- Checklists with useful post-class reference information.
- Any course files you will download.
- The course assessment.
- Notices from the LogicalCHOICE administrator.
- Virtual labs, for remote access to the technical environment for your course.
- Your personal whiteboard for sketches and notes.
- Newsletters and other communications from your learning provider.
- Mentoring services.
- A link to the website of your training provider.
- The LogicalCHOICE store.

Visit your LogicalCHOICE Home screen often to connect, communicate, and extend your learning experience!

How to Use This Book

As You Learn

This book is divided into lessons and topics, covering a subject or a set of related subjects. In most cases, lessons are arranged in order of increasing proficiency.

The results-oriented topics include relevant and supporting information you need to master the content. Each topic has various types of activities designed to enable you to practice the guidelines and procedures as well as to solidify your understanding of the informational material presented in the course. Procedures and guidelines are presented in a concise fashion along with activities and discussions. Information is provided for reference and reflection in such a way as to facilitate understanding and practice.

Data files for various activities as well as other supporting files for the course are available by download from the LogicalCHOICE Course screen. In addition to sample data for the course exercises, the course files may contain media components to enhance your learning and additional reference materials for use both during and after the course.

At the back of the book, you will find a glossary of the definitions of the terms and concepts used throughout the course. You will also find an index to assist in locating information within the instructional components of the book.

As You Review

Any method of instruction is only as effective as the time and effort you, the student, are willing to invest in it. In addition, some of the information that you learn in class may not be important to you immediately, but it may become important later. For this reason, we encourage you to spend some time reviewing the content of the course after your time in the classroom.

As a Reference

The organization and layout of this book make it an easy-to-use resource for future reference. Taking advantage of the glossary, index, and table of contents, you can use this book as a first source of definitions, background information, and summaries.

Course Icons

Watch throughout the material for these visual cues:

Icon	Description
	A **Note** provides additional information, guidance, or hints about a topic or task.
	A **Caution** helps make you aware of places where you need to be particularly careful with your actions, settings, or decisions so that you can be sure to get the desired results of an activity or task.
	LearnTO notes show you where an associated LearnTO is particularly relevant to the content. Access LearnTOs from your LogicalCHOICE Course screen.
	Checklists provide job aids you can use after class as a reference to performing skills back on the job. Access checklists from your LogicalCHOICE Course screen.
	Social notes remind you to check your LogicalCHOICE Course screen for opportunities to interact with the LogicalCHOICE community using social media.
	Notes Pages are intentionally left blank for you to write on.

1 | Getting to Know PCs and the Windows 8.1 User Interface

Lesson Time: 1 hour, 10 minutes

Lesson Objectives

In this lesson, you will get to know PCs and the Windows 8.1 user interface. You will:

*   Identify components of a personal computer.

*   Sign in to Windows 8.1.

*   Explore the Windows 8.1 user interface.

Lesson Introduction

In your office and home, you work with data, communicate with others, research information, and know that computers can help you complete these tasks more quickly and easily. You want to use a computer, but may not know where to start. Using a computer without the basic knowledge of its components and how they work together can be frustrating and can seem complicated. In this lesson, you will identify the components of a personal computer, and examine how these components work together. You will also define fundamental computing concepts and basic computer terms, and sign in to Windows® 8.1. With this knowledge, you'll have a better understanding of how computers work and how they can help you become more efficient in your job.

TOPIC A

Identify Components of a Personal Computer

Identifying the different parts of a personal computer (PC) is a fundamental task. By identifying the different components and becoming more familiar with how they work together, you'll become more comfortable working with PCs, and using them will be more fun.

Personal Computers

PCs have been around since the 1970s. As technology has improved, PCs have gotten smaller and more portable, and the ways they are used more varied. Along with the traditional desktop models, personal computers can now be found in laptop and tablet forms. Because it's inconvenient to carry around a keyboard and a mouse, other input methods have been developed, including voice commands and touch screens.

Unlike a mainframe computer, which is designed to be used simultaneously by many people and requires an operator to oversee its functions, PCs are small, relatively inexpensive machines designed for individual use. They can be used for creating documents, spreadsheets, and databases; or for sending and receiving email; browsing the web; playing games; and a host of other activities. In the business world, PCs can enhance your productivity by enabling you to perform business-related tasks quickly.

Although PCs come in desktop, laptop, and tablet models, they all have certain things in common. Each is made up of three components: hardware, software, and an operating system (OS).

Hardware

The *hardware* of a computer is the physical equipment that you can touch. Hardware includes input devices (such as a keyboard or mouse), processing devices (the system unit), data storage devices (hard drives), and output devices (such as a monitor or printer). On a desktop model, these components are separate units. For laptops and tablets, the monitor, input, and processing devices are all contained in one unit. External data storage devices such as portable hard drives, Secure Digital (SD) cards, or flash drives are also hardware.

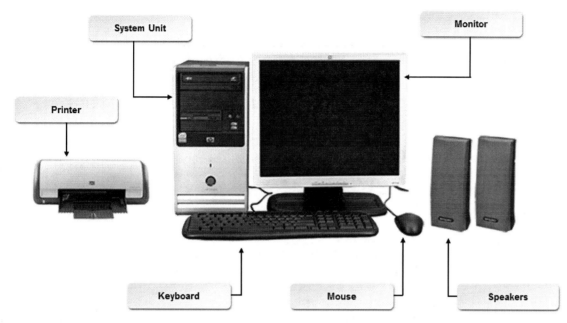

Figure 1–1: A traditional desktop PC. These hardware models are becoming less common with the advent of laptops and mobile devices.

 Note: This course assumes that you are using a PC or tablet with a typical keyboard and mouse. At your job, if you are using a tablet or PC that uses a touch screen, you can use your fingers to make gestures on the display to perform various input tasks.

OS

Computer *software* is a program, or set of instructions, that enables your computer to perform specific tasks. Your computer uses two kinds of software: the *operating system (OS)* and application software. The OS is the most fundamental software that creates the working environment on which application software runs. The OS manages hardware resources by interpreting input from your keyboard, mouse, or touch screen; it stores and retrieves information, and controls output devices such as the monitor or printer. Application programs require an operating system in order to work. Windows 8.1 is an operating system. Other operating systems used on personal computers include Windows 7, Mac® OS X®, and Linux®. Mobile devices such as smartphones have specialized operating systems such as Android™ from Google and iOS from Apple®.

Application Software

Application software (sometimes called simply an "app" on mobile devices such as smartphones and tablet computers) runs on top of the OS and is any program designed to help you perform specific tasks. For example, if you wanted to create a document, you would use a word processor, such as Microsoft Word. There are applications designed to help you to create spreadsheets, develop graphics presentations, track accounting, keep track of your payroll, or browse the Internet. Some applications come preloaded on a new computer; others you can purchase either individually or bundled together. Typical business suite bundles include word processor, spreadsheet, and presentation software.

The following table details common software application types and some example products.

Application	Used For	Examples
Word processor	Creating and editing documents such as letters and reports.	Microsoft Word OpenOffice Writer Corel® WordPerfect® X6
Spreadsheet	Performing accounting tasks and numerical analysis. Set up in table form with rows and columns, each cell in the table can contain text, numbers, or formulas for automatic calculation based on the contents of other cells.	Microsoft Excel® Corel® Quattro® Pro OpenOffice Calc
Database	Organizing and managing large collections of data (information); used for mailing lists, billing, and other activities that require fast sorting or searching through large amounts of information.	Microsoft Access® Oracle® MySQL FileMaker® Pro
Presentation	Visually displaying information. By using graphic images, you can create slide shows, transparencies, posters, and banners. Also used for creating illustrations for use within other documents.	Microsoft PowerPoint® OpenOffice Impress Corel Presentations
Web browser	Searching, retrieving, and viewing documents, videos, images, and other content on the World Wide Web (the Internet).	Microsoft Internet Explorer® Google Chrome™ Mozilla® Firefox®
Email	Sending and receiving digital mail messages over the Internet or other computer networks.	Microsoft Outlook® Yahoo!® Google Gmail™ AOL®
Instant messaging	Exchanging digital, text-based messages in real time over the Internet.	Microsoft Lync® Yahoo! Messenger Google Talk™ AOL Instant Messenger® (AIM®)

ACTIVITY 1-1
Identifying Personal Computer Components and Applications

Scenario

You are the Director of Events for Bit by Bit Fitness, a chain of sporting goods stores founded 25 years ago in Greene City, Richland (RL). Bit by Bit Fitness now has multiple fitness centers in three additional states: Connecticut, New York, and Vermont. Part of your job is coordinating 5K races in the cities in which Bit by Bit Fitness has stores, and keeping tabs on upcoming trends in sportswear. Your team has conducted surveys of your customers, and you want to work with the data gathered. You need to determine what applications you will use to accomplish various tasks as you process the surveys.

 Note: Activities may vary slightly if the software vendor has issued digital updates. Your instructor will notify you of any changes.

 Note: Greene City, RL is a fictional city in a fictional state.

1. How are desktop PCs, laptops, and tablets similar?

2. How are desktop PCs, laptops, and tablets different?

3. What is the purpose of the operating system?
   - ○ To create spreadsheets
   - ○ To create a work environment for application software
   - ○ To process data from a database
   - ○ To share data in documents

4. Which type of software would be best for gathering and sorting through the large amount of data contained in the surveys?
   - ○ Spreadsheet
   - ○ Word processor
   - ○ Database
   - ○ Presentation

5. If you want to type up a report and create a slide show, which two types of software would you likely use?

☐ Spreadsheet

☐ Word processor

☐ Database

☐ Presentation

6. What types of applications might you use for your daily work?

TOPIC B

Sign In to Windows 8.1

Now that you've identified the fundamentals of personal computing, you're ready to start using the Windows 8.1 operating system. You'll begin by entering your unique credentials, which will be the first step in enabling you to use your computer for any number of purposes.

The Boot Process

The first thing you need to do is locate the power button on your computer to turn it on. When you turn on the PC, it performs a series of self-tests to see if everything is in working order; then it loads the OS. This is called *booting* the PC. There are times, such as when software or system updates are needed, when the PC needs to be turned off and on again to apply the updates and go through any necessary clean up procedures. This process of turning the PC off and on again is called a *reboot*.

The Lock Screen

By default, the **Lock** screen is displayed when Windows 8.1 finishes loading, when the PC resumes from sleep mode, or when you need to temporarily secure the PC. The **Lock** screen uses graphics to quickly present information, including the time, date, Internet connection, and notifications from apps such as Mail and Calendar. You don't perform any work on the **Lock** screen—it merely acts as an informative display when you are signed out of your account and the PC is still on.

To save battery life and to prevent unauthorized people from accessing your computer, your PC is set to go into sleep mode, or time out, after being idle for a specified amount of time. When this happens, your account is temporarily locked and the **Lock** screen is displayed. Clicking or tapping anywhere on the screen will take you to the **Sign In** screen, where you can sign in to your account and use your PC.

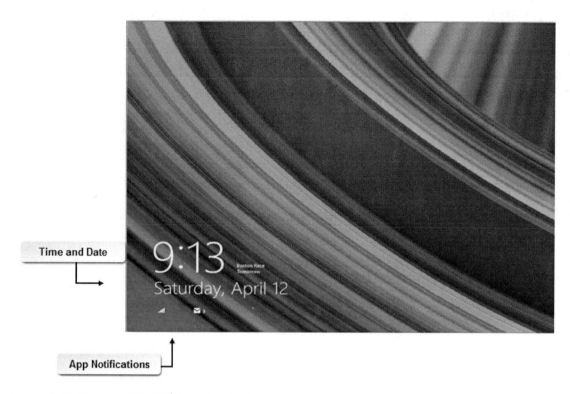

Time and Date

App Notifications

Figure 1-2: One possible Windows 8.1 Lock screen.

The Sign In Screen

Imagine you work in the payroll department. You have a lot of very sensitive data on your PC, and you want to be able to protect that data from people who should not have access to it. By requiring that you enter a password before being able to use the computer, Windows 8.1 provides a means of preventing others from accessing your data. The **Sign In** screen gives you the opportunity to change user accounts (if there are multiple user accounts on the PC), shut the computer down, or turn on accessibility aids to make the computer easier to use.

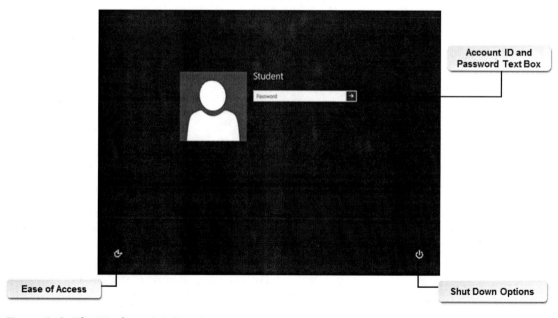

Account ID and Password Text Box

Ease of Access

Shut Down Options

Figure 1-3: The Windows 8.1 Sign In screen.

If more than one person uses a PC, there may be multiple accounts on it, and moving from the **Lock** screen will not take you directly to the **Sign In** screen. Instead, you will see the **Accounts Available** screen, which shows account IDs for all of the accounts on your PC. If this is the case, select the account ID that is associated with your account. This will display the **Sign In** screen for your account.

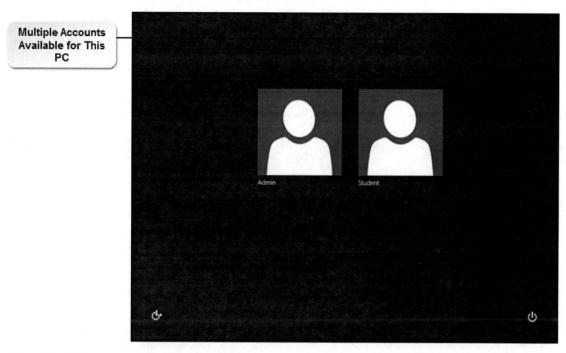

Figure 1-4: The Accounts Available screen.

Ease of Access Menu

The **Ease of Access** menu provides a way to make your computer more accessible through assistive technology. With **Ease of Access**, you can have the **Narrator** feature read aloud the text on your screen, increase the size of the page for readability, turn on an onscreen keyboard, or access other functions that offer alternative methods of making things easier to see and use.

The following table describes the features on the **Ease of Access** menu.

Ease of Access Menu Choice	Description
Narrator	**Narrator** will read aloud what is on the screen, including the text that you are typing, the contents of the active window, and menu options. This option is very helpful for the visually impaired. **Narrator** may not work with all applications.
Magnifier	**Magnifier** will enlarge the whole screen, or portions of the screen, to make viewing easier.
On-Screen Keyboard	Places a virtual keyboard on the screen. Useful for touch screen PCs or when a keyboard is not available.
High Contrast	Provides a darker background to make text and images stand out for better viewing.

Ease of Access Menu Choice	Description
Sticky Keys	Sometimes two or more keys must be pressed at the same time to start an action, such as pressing **Ctrl+Alt+Del** to display **Task Manager** or to cause the computer to reboot. With the **Sticky Keys** feature turned on, you can press the keys in the combination one at a time.
Filter Keys	**Filter Keys** tells the PC how long to respond when a key is pressed and to ignore repeated keystrokes. This is helpful for users who shake, or who have difficulty pressing and lifting their fingers off of keys quickly enough when typing.

Note: To further explore the **Ease of Access** menu, you can access the LearnTO **Use the Magnifier** presentation from the **LearnTO** tile on the LogicalCHOICE Course screen.

Shut Down Options Menu

Turning off your computer incorrectly can result in lost data, damaged files, and damage to your hard drive. When your computer is shut down properly, Windows goes through the process of closing any files it was reading or writing to, ending any processes that were taking place, and properly preparing the hard drive for power loss. The Windows 8.1 **Shut Down** menu offers different options for correctly turning off your computer:

*   **Sleep**—This option is good when you're going to be away from your computer for a short time (for instance, when you're heading out for lunch) and don't want to completely shut the PC down. In sleep mode, your computer turns off the monitor, stops the disk drive, and saves its current state in memory. Sleep mode is a good way to conserve energy and extend the life of your laptop or tablet battery.
*   **Shut Down**—When you are finished with your computer and want to turn it off completely, you should use this option. It allows processes that are taking place to properly close files, store any file that is in memory, run updates, and "clean up" before closing down and turning off the power. In addition to allowing the operating system to properly close out, this option also gives hardware, such as the hard drive, time to prepare before the power is removed.
*   **Restart**—Restart is similar to **Shut Down**, but, instead of ending with the PC turning off, the computer goes through the clean-up process, adds any updates, and then restarts the operating system. Often, when you are loading new software or making changes to settings on your computer, you'll be asked to restart your PC.

Password Sign In

If you have access to the Internet or store valuable company or personal information on your computer, you need to protect it from the many threats in today's world. Hackers, viruses, and thieves are constantly looking to gain access to computers in order to steal information from them. Passwords are one part of the defense available on your PC. The stronger the password, the harder it is for hackers to figure it out. And, like a good lock on your house, the better your password, the more likely the thief is to give up and move on. Microsoft Accounts require passwords to be at least eight characters long, and they must contain at least two of the following: uppercase letters, lowercase letters, numbers, and symbols (for example, & ^ % $ #).

Caution: You should not base passwords on something that is easily found in public records, like your birth date or your children's names. Instead, base your password on a sentence or phrase that you can easily remember. It should contain a combination of upper- and lowercase letters, numbers, and symbols.

Alternative Passwords

Windows 8.1 provides two alternatives to the eight-character-long password. These alternatives can be used on traditional PCs, but they are designed to make signing in on a touch screen easier. The first is the picture password. With this method, you choose a picture and "draw" three gestures on the picture, in any combination of circles, straight lines, and taps. The size and placement of the gestures on the picture become your password.

The second alternative method is a PIN code. This four-digit code is a quick and easy way to sign in to your computer and does not require that you press **Enter** at the end. The PIN is submitted automatically as soon as you put in all four digits. These alternative sign-in methods can be accessed in the PC settings app.

 Access the Checklist tile on your LogicalCHOICE course screen for reference information and job aids on How to Use a Mouse and Sign In to Windows 8.1.

ACTIVITY 1–2
Signing In to Windows 8.1

Before You Begin

Your instructor will provide you with a user account for your Windows 8.1 system. Write down your user ID and password.

User ID: _____

Password: **win8class**

Scenario

It's 8 A.M. and you've just arrived in the office. You want to sign in to the computer and begin your day. You get your coffee and sit down at your computer.

---

1. Turn on your computer.
   a) Locate and press the power button.
   b) Verify that the computer starts up.

2. Sign in to Windows 8.1.
   a) On the **Lock** screen, click or tap anywhere on the screen, or swipe up to move to the next screen.
   b) Once you have reached the **Sign In** screen, in the **Password** text box, type *win8class* and then press **Enter**.

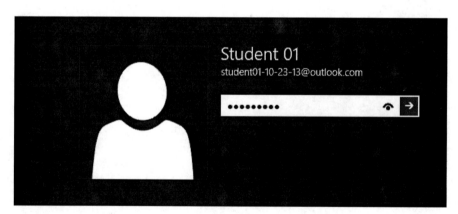

TOPIC C

Navigate the Start Screen

So far, you have identified personal computer hardware and types of software, and signed in to Windows 8.1. Now you're ready to start putting Windows 8.1 to work for you.

The Start Screen

The **Start** screen is the central user interface of Windows 8.1 and acts as the hub from which you can access all of the capabilities of your computer. From the **Start** screen, you can run programs, check your email, add contacts, see the latest news, get updates on the weather, change the settings on your PC, sign out of your computer, go online, and much more.

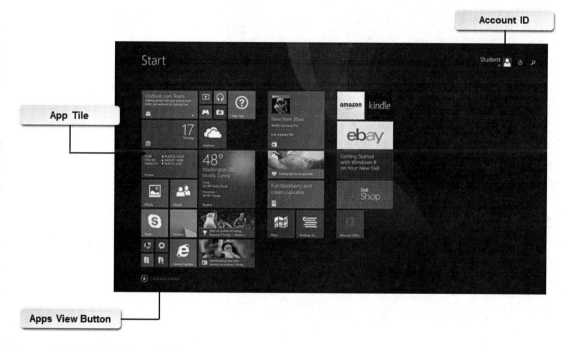

Figure 1-5: The Windows 8.1 Start screen.

Sign in to Desktop

Windows 8.1 can be configured to boot directly to the Desktop or to the **Start** screen. Depending on how your computer is configured, you might see the Desktop when you sign in instead of seeing the **Start** screen. You can configure which option you prefer to see upon sign in.

 Access the Checklist tile on your LogicalCHOICE course screen for reference information and job aids on How to Boot to Start.

Tiles

The first thing you'll notice about the **Start** screen is that it has colorful squares and rectangles displayed, each with a different name and picture, or icon. These colorful objects are called *tiles*, and each tile represents a different app or link to a website. The tiles aren't actually the apps themselves, but act as a shortcut or quick way of accessing an app. For instance, if you select the **Calendar** tile, it will run the Calendar app. If you select the **Weather** tile, you'll be taken online to view weather in any city you choose. Applications written in the new Windows 8.1 user interface are called *Windows Store apps*, whereas traditional software programs written for previous Windows OS versions are called *Desktop applications*. Windows 8.1 supports both types of software, with traditional applications running on the Desktop OS app.

 Note: To learn how to access more apps than what come packaged with Windows 8.1, you can access the LearnTO **Download Apps from the Windows Store** presentation from the **LearnTO** tile on the LogicalCHOICE Course screen.

Tooltips

If the name of the app is not displayed on the tile, you can hold your pointer over the tile and a *tooltip* will display the name of the app. Windows 8.1 also provides tooltips for icons in many of the apps.

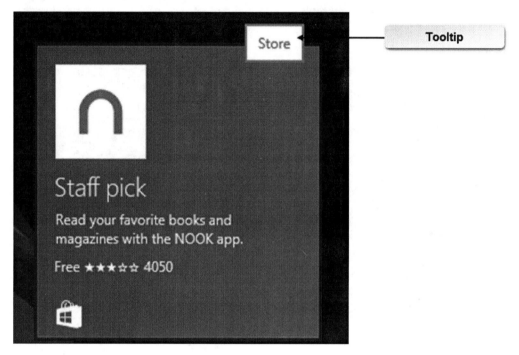

Figure 1-6: The Store tile with its tooltip.

Tile Position

As you work with Windows 8.1, you may find that you use some tiles more than others, or that, as you add more apps, you have so many tiles that you can't find anything. You can easily move a tile by *dragging* it to a new position. The other tiles will move to accommodate the space left by the tile you moved.

 Caution: Be careful when dragging tiles. If you press the mouse button but do not hold it down, the tile will open the app associated with it.

Live Tiles

Some tiles do more than just run apps. *Live tiles* can display real-time information, even when the app isn't running. For example, the **Finance** tile will display current stock market coverage, along with breaking financial news; the **Calendar** tile will display upcoming appointments; and the **Mail** tile will show how many unread email messages you have.

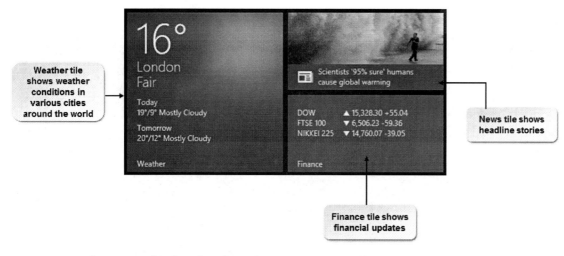

Figure 1–7: Information displayed on live tiles.

The App Command Bar

The app command bar is hidden on the bottom of the screen and contains options for managing the tiles that are currently shown on, or pinned to, the **Start** screen. With this command bar, you can turn a live tile on or off, unpin a tile from **Start**, uninstall an app, and change the size of a tile. With the command bar activated on the **Start** screen, you may also name groups of tiles to your liking. Right-click the desired tile to view its app command bar.

On Windows 8.1 computers where the primary input is keyboard and mouse rather than touch, instead of showing the app command bar, when you right-click a tile on the **Start** screen, a menu is displayed next to the tile instead. The same options are listed on the menu that would be listed on the app command bar. On these systems, if you want to display the app command bar, press **Windows key+Z**.

Figure 1–8: Tile management tools on the app command bar.

Start Button

You can return to the **Start** screen at any time, from any screen, by using the **Start** button. To access the **Start** button, move your pointer to the lower-left corner of your screen and select the tiny Windows icon that appears. The **Start** button is available whenever you have navigated away from the **Start** screen. When you are on the **Start** screen, the **Start** button will take you back to the previous app you were using. If you have no apps open, the **Start** button will not appear on the **Start** screen.

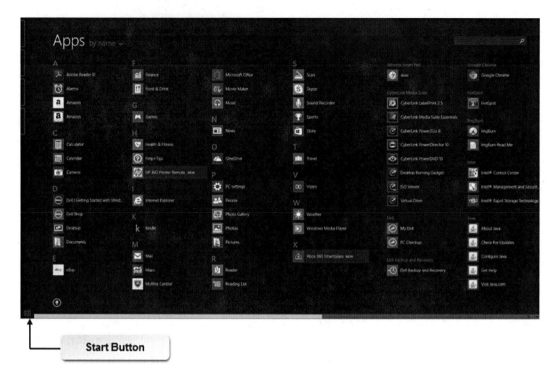

Figure 1-9: The Start button.

The Scroll Bar

The **Start** screen can hold more tiles than can be viewed on one page. You can scroll the **Start** screen to view all of the tiles pinned on it by using the scroll bar at the bottom of the screen. To display the scroll bar, just move the pointer and it will appear. The scroll bar has arrows on each end for slow scrolling, and a slider bar that you can drag for faster scrolling.

Figure 1-10: The scroll bar at the bottom of the Start screen.

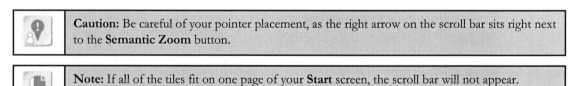

Caution: Be careful of your pointer placement, as the right arrow on the scroll bar sits right next to the **Semantic Zoom** button.

Note: If all of the tiles fit on one page of your **Start** screen, the scroll bar will not appear.

Access the Checklist tile on your LogicalCHOICE course screen for reference information and job aids on How to Manage Tiles on the Start Screen.

ACTIVITY 1–3
Managing Tiles

Before You Begin
You are signed in to your account and are viewing the **Start** screen.

Scenario
You've been working with Windows 8.1 at your job for a while now. You really like it, but you'd like to make the tiles easier to find, and you do not need all of the tiles pinned to the **Start** screen. You decide that taking a few minutes to manage your tiles now will save you a lot of time in your day-to-day work. Because you know you'll be too busy to use your computer for games, and don't have much use for maps, you can unpin those tiles from the **Start** screen. You use **Calendar** often, so you decide to make it larger. It would be nice to be able to do calculations without having to get your calculator out, and you remember seeing a calculator program on the **All Apps** screen, so you decide to pin the calculator to the **Start** screen so it's always handy. Let's get started and do some housekeeping.

1. Unpin tiles from the **Start** screen.
   a) Right-click the **Games** tile.
      The pop-up menu is displayed or the app command bar appears across the bottom of your screen.
   b) Select **Unpin from Start**.
   c) Unpin the **Maps** tile from the **Start** screen.
   d) Ensure the **Games** and **Maps** tiles no longer appear on the **Start** screen.

2. Change the size of a tile and move it.
   a) Right-click the **Calendar** tile.

   b) Select **Resize**.
   c) Select **Large**.

d) Click and drag the **Calendar** tile below **Finance**.

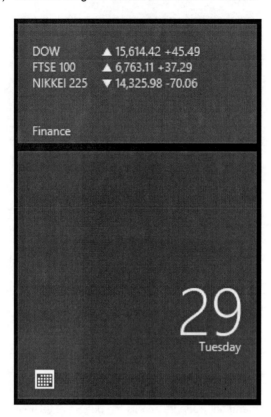

e) If necessary, select anywhere on the **Start** screen background to return to the default view.

3. Pin an app to the **Start** screen.
   a) From the **Start** screen, select the **Apps View** down-arrow button.
   b) Under the **Windows Accessories** group of programs, find **Calculator** and right-click it.

c) Select **Pin to Start**.
d) Verify that you automatically return to the **Start** screen.

4. Verify that the **Calculator** tile is now pinned to the **Start** screen.

5. If the scroll bar appears, move it all the way to the left to display the beginning of the **Start** screen.

Account ID

On the top-right corner of the **Start** screen is your **Account ID**, featuring your picture and name. There may be times when you'll be sharing a computer with someone else; for instance, if your work takes you out in the field a lot, the company may supply a shared PC for those infrequent times that you and your coworkers are in the office, and each of you would be assigned an account. This enables you to customize your account with only those apps that pertain to your work, and protects your data from being changed or deleted by others. Although only one account would be active at a time, multiple people can be signed in to the computer at the same time. In these instances, it's important to know that you are using the correct account. The **Account ID** tells you whose account is currently active on the PC.

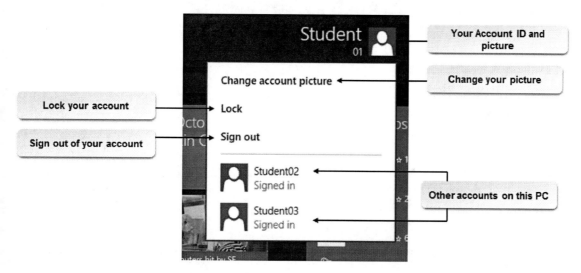

Figure 1-11: The Account ID menu.

Account ID Menu Options

By selecting the **Account ID**, you can access the **Account ID** menu, where you can change your account picture, lock your account, sign out of the computer, or change user accounts.

Account ID Menu Item	Description
Change account picture	Takes you to the **Accounts** menu of the **PC settings** page, where you can select a picture from your files, or use the camera on your PC to create a picture as your ID.
Lock	Leaves everything running on your account, but brings you to the **Lock** screen and locks your account. Your account cannot be accessed until your password is entered on the **Sign In** screen. Other accounts may be used while your account is locked.
Sign out	Closes all programs and files you have open and signs you out of the computer, ending your session. The PC remains on.
Other user **Account ID(s)**	Locks your account and lets other users sign in under their accounts.

 Access the Checklist tile on your LogicalCHOICE course screen for reference information and job aids on How to Lock Your Account and Sign Out of Windows 8.1.

ACTIVITY 1-4
Using the Account ID Menu

Before You Begin
You are viewing the **Start** screen.

Scenario
It's lunch time, and you're about to head out to grab a bite to eat. Because you'll be away from your desk for an hour, you want to lock your computer while leaving it running. When you return, you'll sign back in and complete your work for the day. A few hours later, it's the end of the day, and you are ready to head home. Your company wants to save energy and has asked everyone to turn their computers off at night, so you'll want to shut yours down properly. The next morning, you'll start a new day by turning your PC back on and signing in.

---

1. Lock your account, and then sign back in.
   a) In the upper right of your screen, select your **Account ID**.
   b) From the menu, select **Lock**. Your account will be locked and you will be taken to the **Lock** screen.

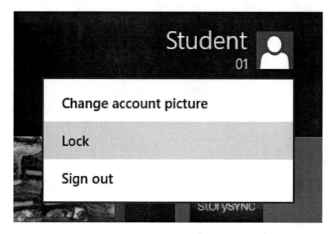

   c) At the **Lock** screen, select anywhere, or swipe up to move to the next screen.
   d) On the **Sign In** screen, in the **Password** text box, type *win8class* and press **Enter**.

2. Shut down the computer.
   a) In the upper right of your screen, select your **Account ID**.
   b) From the menu, select **Sign out**.
   c) At the **Lock** screen, select anywhere to get to the **Sign In** screen.
   d) At the **Sign In** screen, select the **Shut down** icon.

   e) From the **Shut down** menu, select **Shut down**.
   f) Verify that the shutdown process is completed.

3. Turn on your computer and sign in.

    a) Locate and press the power button.

    b) Verify that the computer goes through the startup process.

    c) Sign in to Windows 8.1.

Summary

In this lesson, you identified PC hardware and software basics, signed in to Windows 8.1, and worked with the new Windows user interface (UI). With this basic knowledge and skill, you're ready to start working with Windows 8.1.

Why do you think Microsoft Accounts require passwords to contain at least two of the following: uppercase letters, lowercase letters, numbers, and symbols? How does this benefit you?

In what ways will you use the Start screen for your benefit?

 Note: Check your LogicalCHOICE Course screen for opportunities to interact with your classmates, peers, and the larger LogicalCHOICE online community about the topics covered in this course or other topics you are interested in. From the Course screen you can also access available resources for a more continuous learning experience.

2 | Using Windows Store Apps and Navigation Features

Lesson Time: 1 hour

Lesson Objectives

In this lesson, you will use Windows Store apps and navigation features. You will:

- Identify the Charms and use them with various apps.
- Use the Windows 8.1 **Start** screen to open apps and navigate in them.
- Navigate between Store apps.

Lesson Introduction

Now that you've seen the Microsoft® Windows® 8.1 user interface (UI) and explored the **Start** screen, it's time to use a few of the Store apps that come bundled with Windows 8.1 and navigate within and between them. Using these apps to accomplish the various tasks you need to perform will make your job easier.

TOPIC A

Access and Identify the Charms

One of the design features of Windows 8.1 is ease of use. With the Charms, you have universal access to common tools no matter where you are in Windows 8.1. The Charms will make working within and between apps much easier.

The Charms

Hidden on the right side of the screen are the *Charms*. The Charms are universal tools that are available from everywhere in Windows 8.1, and give you access to key system-wide functions such as printing, searching, and sharing. Some Charms are dynamic and context sensitive; for instance, using the **Settings Charm** within the **Photos** app will give you the option of changing how images are displayed in this app; using **Settings** from the **Start** screen allows you to change how the **Start** screen is presented.

Bringing up the Charms also brings up a display showing the current date and time, along with Internet connectivity strength. If you are using a laptop or tablet, it will also display battery life.

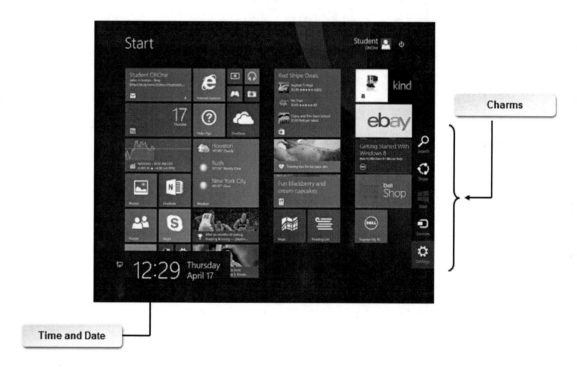

Figure 2-1: The Charms available on the Start screen.

Functions of the Charms

The following table describes the Charms available on the **Start** screen.

Charm	Function
Search	The **Search Charm** allows you to search for apps, settings, files, or online terms. This is an aggregated search that defaults to displaying results for all of these categories at once. The **Search** menu indicates where you will be searching by listing the targeted search area above the **Search** text box. The menu also displays suggestions below the **Search** text box. You can select these suggestions to begin the search or start the app. Windows 8.1 saves your search phrases for use in future searches and displays them under the **Search** text box. Select one of these for faster searching.
Share	The **Share Charm** allows you to share data via Mail. Share is fully functional only with Store apps that have the necessary permission; Desktop apps are limited to sharing a screenshot of what is currently being displayed. The options for sharing vary by app and the type of data you are sharing.
Start	The **Start Charm** works the same way as the **Start** button and returns you to the **Start** screen from any app. Or, if you are at the **Start** screen, it will return you to the last open app you were using.
Devices	The **Devices Charm** allows you to interact with the devices connected to your PC. Using this Charm, you can connect to other devices, choose a printer and print from any Store app, stream media and other content to external devices, and configure the monitors connected to your PC. This last option is helpful when you are working with dual monitors.
Settings	The **Settings Charm** is also context sensitive, and options vary among apps. On **Start**, it allows you to access **Help** and **PC settings**, clear any personal information from live tiles, connect to and check on the strength of your Internet connection, adjust speaker volume, change the brightness of your screen, display an onscreen keyboard, and hide notifications. This charm also enables you to access the power menu to shut down, restart, or put your PC in sleep mode.

 Access the Checklist tile on your LogicalCHOICE course screen for reference information and job aids on How to Access the Charms.

ACTIVITY 2-1
Using the Charms

Before You Begin
You are viewing the **Start** screen.

Scenario
You've been working with Windows 8.1 at your job for a few days now, and although you're enjoying the experience for the most part, there is one thing that annoys you: sound. You work in a relatively quiet office next to several other people that are part of your team, and you don't want to keep disturbing them with the sounds that occasionally play from your computer. You've tried looking for a way to turn off the sound from the **Start** screen and the **Apps View** screen, but you can't find a specific app for this purpose. Remembering that you can quickly search your entire computer from the Charms, you decide to use its universal search function to find speaker settings. When that fails to turn up what you're looking for, you realize that there are miscellaneous system settings you can also access from the Charms, so you try that.

---

1. Access the Charms.

    a) Move your pointer to the top right of your screen until the charms appear, and then slide the pointer down the right side of the screen until the Charms become active.

     Note: If the Charms don't appear, pull your pointer away from the right side and try again. Do not press any of the mouse buttons while you're doing this.

    b) Slide your pointer over the **Search Charm** to highlight it.

2. Search for speaker settings.

    a) Select the **Search Charm**.
    b) Verify that you are taken to the **Search** pane.
    c) In the **Search** box, enter *Speakers* and as you type, observe how the suggestions listed below the **Search** box change as you enter each letter.

d) Verify that no apps are listed, only similar search terms.

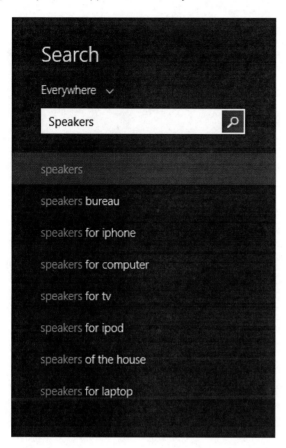

e) Select outside of the **Search** pane on the **Start** screen to close it.

3. Mute your computer's speakers.
   a) Display the Charms.

b) Select the **Settings Charm** to display the **Settings** pane.

c) At the bottom of the **Settings** pane, select the speaker icon.

d) If necessary, from the volume menu that pops up, select the black speaker icon to mute your speakers.

The speaker icon on the **Settings** pane changes to include an "X" and is labeled **Muted**.

e) Select outside of the **Settings** pane on the **Start** screen to close it.

TOPIC B

Windows Store Apps and Common Navigation Features

Now that you've accessed the helpful Charms feature, it's time to get into what you'll likely be using the most: apps. Apps geared toward the Windows 8.1 operating system are designed to look and behave in similar ways, which will help streamline your workflow and increase productivity. In this topic, you'll work with an app to access a variety of useful information quickly and easily.

Windows Store Apps

Windows 8.1 comes preloaded with several simple apps that can be useful and give you a good idea of how Store apps work. Some of these apps include Mail, Calendar, People, Maps, Weather, and News. To start an app, select the tile associated with it.

 Note: You might also hear Windows Store apps referred to as Modern apps or Windows 8-style apps.

You can obtain additional apps from the Windows Store. Select the **Store** tile on the **Start** screen to access the Windows Store. Some of these apps are free and others require payment. The price is listed with the app in the Store. If it is free, the price will be listed as Free.

Common Windows Store App Navigation Features

Store apps have several common navigation features, including scroll bars, app command bars, **Next Page** and **Previous Page** arrows, a **Back** arrow, onscreen content icons, and the Charms. As with the **Start** screen, apps use scroll bars so you can view content that can't fit on one screen. Some apps have scroll bars along the right side for vertical scrolling, or along the bottom for horizontal scrolling.

Figure 2–2: Page navigation features within the Finance app.

You can also access app command bars by right-clicking the page background or a specific item on the screen. App command bars can appear at the top as well as the bottom of the screen. Command bar options vary according to the app in which they appear. However, most follow the same basic template: the top bar displays navigation controls, the bottom left of the command bar is reserved for contextual actions, and the bottom right options stay the same within the app.

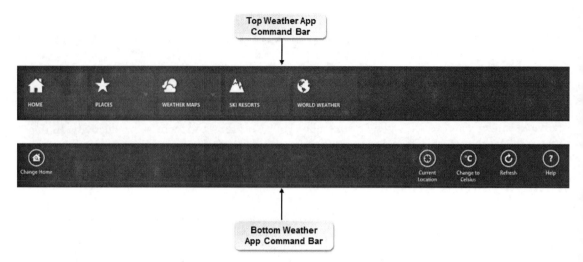

Figure 2–3: The top and bottom app command bars within the Weather app.

Apps often have interactive icons and tiles that change the contents of the page or reveal more information. For instance, the Weather app displays a chart that will show historical temperature, rainfall, or snow days, depending on which icon you select. Some in-app icons, when selected, will display time-elapsed weather conditions such as temperature and cloud cover. You can also find small arrows within the page that hide or reveal more information.

 Access the Checklist tile on your LogicalCHOICE course screen for reference information and job aids on How to Open a Windows Store App and Use Navigation Features.

ACTIVITY 2-2
Navigating a Windows Store App

Scenario

Bit by Bit is hosting a 5K race this weekend in Danbury, CT. Because weather has a big impact on the runners and vendors, you need to be aware of any impending problems and plan accordingly. You're currently in another city, so you need to go online to check the weather forecast in Danbury to see if you'll have to order extra tents. You'd also like to check the weather in New York City for a sporting goods convention you'll be attending there tomorrow.

---

1. Open the Weather app.
    a) On the **Start** screen, select the **Weather** tile. The Weather app opens.
    b) Verify that the **Weather** screen comes up displaying the weather where you are.

2. Search for a location.
    a) In the upper-right corner of the screen, select the **Search** button.

    b) Verify that the insertion point is flashing in this text box, indicating that any text you type will be entered here.
    c) In the **Search** text box, enter *Danbury* and examine the suggested locations listed below the text box as you type. Confirm that the results are refined as you get more specific.
    d) When it shows in the list below the text box, select **Danbury Connecticut, United States**.

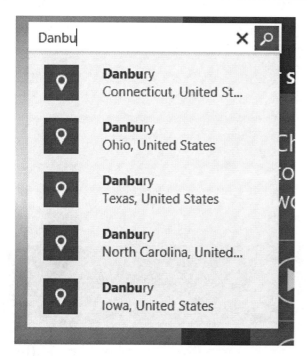

    e) In the Weather app, verify that Danbury, CT, weather is displayed.

3. Use navigation icons.

a)

> **Note:** Depending on whether you have a wide-screen monitor (16:9 ratio) or square monitor(4;3 ratio), the multi-day forecast will be displayed differently. The steps here assume you are using a wide-screen monitor. On a square monitor, the multi-day forecast is listed vertically with a scrollbar to the right to see additional days.

Select the right arrow to the right of the multi-day forecast to reveal forecasts for the next several days.

b) Verify that the arrow now points to the left. This signifies that selecting it will scroll to the left, going back to the first five days of forecasts.

c) Select the arrow and confirm that the first days of the forecast are displayed again.

d) Below the right arrow, select the up arrow.

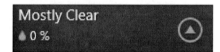

e) Verify that more information is revealed below the five-day forecast.

f) Confirm that the arrow now points down.

g) Select the down arrow to hide the additional information.

4. Access the command bars.

a) Right-click the page. Verify that the top and bottom app command bars are displayed.

b) Examine the options in the navigation bar at the top.

c) Select **WORLD WEATHER** to display an interactive page showing the current weather in cities across the world.

5. Use interactive navigation features.
   a) Select a land area.
      The map zooms in on that area and weather is displayed for cities in that region.
   b) Select the map again to zoom back out.
   c) Select the **New York City** weather label. Confirm the weather is displayed for New York City.

6. Navigate to the previous page.
   a) In the top-left corner, select the **Back** arrow to go back a page.
   b) Repeat until you are back to the Danbury weather page.

7. Set a default Weather home page.
   a) From the app command bar, select **PLACES**. Verify that Danbury is listed as a recent weather search.
   b) Select the **Danbury** tile to go to its page.

FAVORITES

RECENT SEARCHES

   c) Right-click, and on the bottom command bar, select **Set as Home**.

8. Add a favorite place.
   a) Return to the **PLACES** page from the command bar.
   b) Select the black tile containing a plus sign.
   c) In the text box that appears, enter **New York City** and select **New York City, New York, United States**.
   d) Under **Favorites**, verify that New York City is now listed.

9. Select the Danbury tile to return to the default Weather page.

10. Move your pointer to the bottom-left corner of the screen and select the **Start** button to return to the **Start** screen.

TOPIC C

Multitask with Apps

In your daily work, you probably won't be using one program at a time, but will open multiple programs to reference information from one program for use in another, or to multitask for more efficiency. With this in mind, Windows 8.1 was designed to make moving from one app to another easy.

Multiple-App Functionality

It's often useful to work with multiple apps, such as when you are referring to information in one app for use in another, or when you are called away from the document you are working on to display information for a coworker. Windows 8.1 supports running more than one app at a time, and Store apps are designed to work together. The method for opening a second app is the same as opening the first: selecting the appropriate tile on the **Start** screen. The app you are currently working with typically runs in the foreground, covering the entire screen, while any other open app is suspended in the background to conserve energy. When you switch to the suspended app, it instantly resumes running, and the app you were working with is suspended. There are exceptions to this rule. For instance, the Music app continues running in the background so that you can listen to music as you work. Windows 8.1 also provides for viewing up to eight apps at the same time.

The Switcher

When you have more than one app running at a time, the *Switcher* lets you flip between them. Hidden in the top-left corner of your screen, the **Switcher** will show a tile of the previous app you were working with. Select the tile to switch to the suspended app. If there are more than two apps running, you can select the **Switcher** multiple times until you get to the desired app, or you can slide your pointer down the left side to expand the **Switcher** and display tiles for all apps that are currently open. Select any of these to resume working in the app represented by that tile.

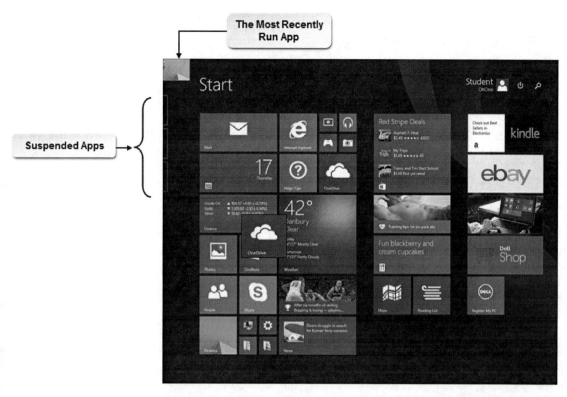

Figure 2-4: The Switcher showing the Desktop tile with other apps suspended in the background.

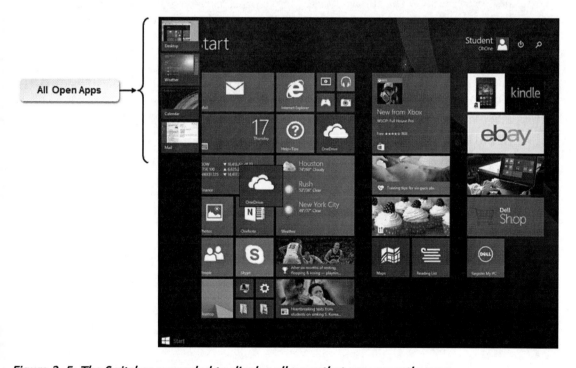

Figure 2-5: The Switcher expanded to display all apps that are currently open.

The Close App Function

Because Windows 8.1 suspends apps when they are not in use and will close them automatically, you don't need to close an app when you're finished with it. However, having too many apps open at once can make switching between apps cumbersome, so it may be easier to close any apps that you no longer need. There are two ways to close an app. You can move your pointer to the top of the screen and "drag" the app off the bottom of the screen, or you can use the **Switcher** to view the app tile, right-click the tile, and select **Close**.

Close an Active Window

You can close the active window using a variety of methods. You can drag the window down from the top until it shrinks to a smaller rectangle, then drag it off the bottom of the screen. You can also hover the mouse near the top of the active window until a title bar appears with the name of the window in the center. A **Close** button (**X**) is displayed on the right side of the title bar. Selecting the **Close** button will also close the active window. Yet another method of closing the active window is using the traditional keyboard shortcut **Alt + F4**.

Close All Processes for an App

When you close a Windows Store app, portions of the app remain running in the background. This makes it faster to reopen a closed app. Windows will eventually close the app and all processes if the memory is needed. If you want to completely close all of the processes for an app, you can drag the app off the bottom of the screen, then up slightly until the image "flips" or use **Task Manager** on the Desktop to close the app and all of its processes.

The Snap Feature

There may be instances when you'll want to view multiple apps at the same time. Perhaps you're working with figures on a spreadsheet and need to include some of these in a report or email. Rather than having to remember the numbers as you flip between the apps, you can use the *Snap* feature to show multiple apps on the screen together. To do this, just move your pointer to the top of the page and drag the app to the side. The app will "snap" into a pane, leaving a second pane to display another app. Use the **Switcher** to put the second app into the other pane. Both apps will default to covering half of the page. You can easily change these proportions by dragging the *snap bar* to the left or right, as needed. However, different apps require a different minimum amount of space, so you may be unable to achieve a 90 to 10 percent screen proportion, for example. To return any app to suspension and display only one app on your screen, drag the snap bar all the way to the left or right, covering up the app you wish to suspend. Depending on your monitor's screen resolution, you may have up to four apps snapped at once, and up to eight if you connect two monitors at sufficient resolution.

One app shows in
the left pane

The other app shows
in the right pane

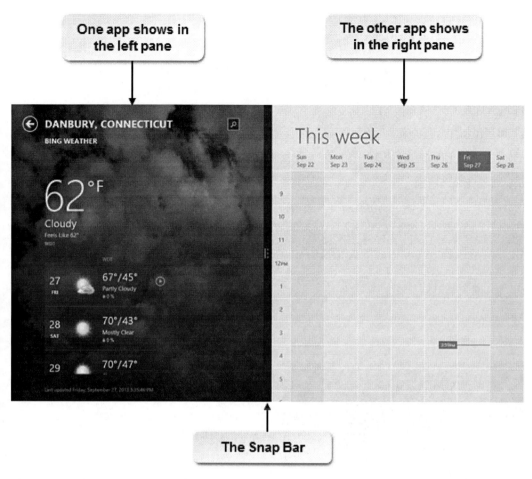

The Snap Bar

Figure 2-6: Two apps snapped.

 Access the Checklist tile on your LogicalCHOICE course screen for reference
information and job aids on How to Multitask with Apps.

ACTIVITY 2–3
Working with Multiple Apps

Before You Begin
The Weather app is active, but suspended. You are viewing the **Start** screen.

Scenario
Your company has another event in Boston after the Danbury race, and you may schedule post-race events there if weather permits. You can work with both apps at the same time to check the weather and schedule the days on your calendar. You will open the Calendar app and use the Snap feature to view both apps at once. When you're finished with the Weather app, you'll put the Calendar back on full screen.

---

1. Open the Calendar app.
    a) Select the **Calendar** tile to open the app.

    b) Right-click on the page to open the command bar.
    c) From the top, select **Week** to open a layout of the whole week. Spaces for each day are large enough to show appointments, and the current day is highlighted in dark gray.

2. Snap the Calendar app.
    a) Move your pointer to the top of the Calendar page
    b) Drag the Calendar to the right of the screen.
    c) When the snap bar appears, let go.
        The Calendar app snaps to the right pane.

3. Use the **Switcher** to access the Weather app and snap it.
    a) Move your pointer to the upper-left corner of the screen until the **Switcher** tile appears. It will show a preview of what the snapped apps will look like.
    b) Select the tile to activate the Weather app.

c) Verify the Weather app snaps into the pane on the left side of the screen.

4. Search for a location in Weather.
   a) Using the **Search** button in the **Weather** app, search for *Boston*

   b) Select **Boston Massachusetts, United States**.
   c) Verify that the Weather app now shows weather for Boston, MA.
   d) If necessary, use the scroll bar arrows at the right of the Weather forecast to view more of the screen so you can scroll through the weather for upcoming days.

5. Add events to the Calendar.
   a) Right-click the Calendar.
   b) Select the **New** icon that appears at the bottom-right of the **Calendar** screen.
   c) In the **Subject** text box, type *Boston race*

   d) Select the **When** box and change the day to next Sunday.

e) Select the **How long** box and select **Custom**.

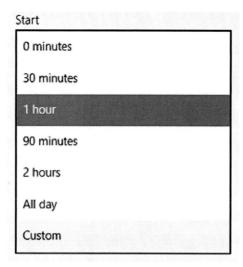

Start

0 minutes

30 minutes

1 hour

90 minutes

2 hours

All day

Custom

New options appear.

f) For the **Start** date, check the **All day** check box.

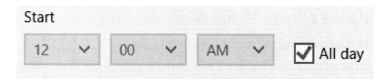

Start

| 12 ∨ | 00 ∨ | AM ∨ | ☑ All day |

The **Start** and **End** times gray out.

g) Select the **End** date box and then, from the calendar, select the following Wednesday.

 Note: The list will show only the days for the current month. You may have to advance the month if the following Wednesday is in the next month.

h) From the top-right of the **Calendar** screen, select the **Save this event** button.

Save this event (Ctrl+S)

←

Student's calendar
student01-09-25-13@outlook.com

Subject

Boston race

i) Verify that there is now a line labeled **Boston race** over the four days of your new event.

	Sun Sep 29	Mon Sep 30	Tue Oct 1	Wed Oct 2	Thu Oct 3
	Boston...	Boston...	Boston...	Boston...	
9					
10					
11					

 Note: As in the previous screenshot, the full text of the event might not appear due to the current proportions of your snapped apps.

6. Change the snap proportions.
    a) Move your pointer over the snap bar and drag the bar to the left until the Weather app occupies a smaller section of the screen and the Calendar app occupies a larger section.
    b) Examine the Calendar and confirm that your **Boston race** event is displayed fully across the designated days.

7. Return the Calendar to full-screen mode.
    a) Move your pointer over the snap bar and drag the bar off to the left of the screen.
        The Weather app disappears and is suspended.
    b) Verify that the Calendar covers the entire screen and your **Boston race** appointment spans the Calendar from Sunday to Wednesday.

8. Access the **Switcher** to view open apps.
    a) Return to the **Start** screen.
    b) On the **Start** screen, move your pointer to the upper-left corner of the screen and slide it down the left side. All the open apps are displayed. In this case, you have the Calendar and Weather apps open.
    c) Move your pointer away from the **Switcher** to close it.

Summary

In this lesson, you used the **Start** screen to open an app, navigated around and entered text in an app, and worked with two apps at once by using Snap and the **Switcher**. You also used the Charms to access common app features with ease. With these tools, you'll be able to open and work with the various apps you'll need.

How might the Charms improve your productivity at work?

How might you use multiple apps at once?

 Note: Check your LogicalCHOICE Course screen for opportunities to interact with your classmates, peers, and the larger LogicalCHOICE online community about the topics covered in this course or other topics you are interested in. From the Course screen you can also access available resources for a more continuous learning experience.

3 | Working with Desktop Applications

Lesson Time: 1 hour, 30 minutes

Lesson Objectives

In this lesson, you will work with Desktop applications. You will:

- Navigate the Desktop app interface.

- Manage files and folders.

- Identify elements of a Desktop window.

- Use a Desktop application to create and modify a file.

Lesson Introduction

Now that you've worked with two Microsoft® Windows® 8.1 Store apps, Calendar and Weather, let's take a look at the Desktop and work with some classic applications. Because the Windows 8.1 user interface (UI) is so new, most of the applications you will be using will still be run on the classic Desktop environment. Becoming familiar with the Desktop and classic applications is essential to using a PC in your day-to-day work. This lesson introduces some of the basic concepts of the Desktop, files and folders, and explores the navigation features common to Desktop applications. You will be able to create and modify documents and keep your work on the PC organized.

TOPIC A

Navigate the Desktop

The Desktop has several features, some similar to the **Start** screen, that will help you navigate its environment. Before you dive into Desktop apps themselves, you'll want to access these features so you'll have an easier time getting to where you need to go. In this topic, you'll find and access some of the more common Desktop interface elements.

The Desktop

In a typical office, two main components facilitate work: the filing cabinet and the desktop. You store and organize things in your filing cabinets, and do your work on your desktop. In earlier, or "classic," Windows operating system versions, the Desktop was the central place on your computer where you did your work. When you opened a program or a file, it would run on the Desktop. You may have a lot of things on your desk at work, but your desktop is still there, underneath. So it is with the Desktop on your PC. In Windows 8.1, the **Start** screen is the central place from which you open programs on your computer. However, because there are so many applications that still run only in the classic Desktop environment, Windows 8.1 provides the *Desktop* operating system as an app. You may even choose to go directly to the Desktop instead of the **Start** screen when you sign in to your computer.

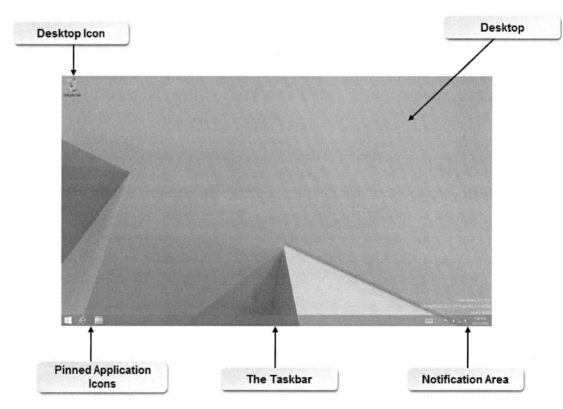

Figure 3-1: The Desktop.

The Taskbar

The *taskbar* runs along the bottom of the screen and, like the **Start** screen, it can have common applications pinned to it for easier access. The taskbar has several functions; one of which is to display icons for those applications that are currently running. Selecting these icons enables you to switch back and forth between the open applications. Some applications allow you to have multiple files open. When this happens, you will see what looks like overlapping icons on the taskbar. Select this multi-icon to view, switch to, or close the files that are open using that application. The taskbar also displays Internet access and signal strength, whether or not speakers are enabled, and notifications for software updates and system problems, among other things. An always-visible **Start** button allows you to quickly return to the **Start** screen. While the default placement is along the bottom of the screen, you can move the taskbar to any edge of the screen, or set it to hide when not in use.

The taskbar is available on both the Desktop and on the **Start** screen. On the Desktop, it is visible by default unless you select the option to auto-hide it. On the **Start** screen, it is visible if you move your mouse pointer off the bottom of the screen.

The Notification Area

The *Notification area* is located on the right side of the taskbar. By default, this area displays icons for system functions, and each icon enables you to execute a different type of system command, such as safely removing external memory storage devices, connecting to the Internet and determining signal strength, managing speaker volume, and viewing battery life on laptops and other portable devices. There is also an icon that displays a preview of the Action Center, which shows notification issues with your computer or software updates. The Notification area is customizable, so you can add or remove icons and adjust the notification behaviors of each.

Tooltips

Just as with Windows Store apps, if you place your pointer over an icon or menu choice on the Desktop or in an application, a tooltip will appear. Tooltips display the application name or a brief description of what that application or menu choice will do.

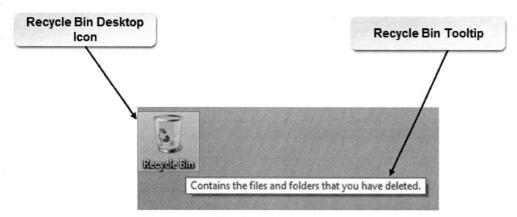

Figure 3–2: The tooltip for the Recycle Bin.

Context Menus

Context menus, also called jump lists, provide quick access to common tasks associated with different applications. When you right-click an icon, the taskbar, or the Desktop itself, a context menu will display files frequently used or recently accessed by the application, and tasks that can be performed with that application. Some examples of tasks found on context menus include opening the application, opening the application to view a file listed on the context menu, and pinning or unpinning the application from the taskbar or **Start** screen. Some context menus show *keyboard shortcuts* associated with the tasks displayed. Keyboard shortcuts are keys or a combination of keys which, when pressed together or in succession, will execute a command that is otherwise executed by opening a menu or using a pointer. Keyboard shortcuts can increase efficiency by reducing the need to lift your hands from the keyboard in order to use the mouse to execute a command. Although not all of them will apply to Windows 8.1, you can find a complete list of keyboard shortcuts for Windows on the Microsoft Windows website at **http:// windows.microsoft.com/en-us/windows/keyboard-shortcuts#keyboard-shortcuts=windows-8**.

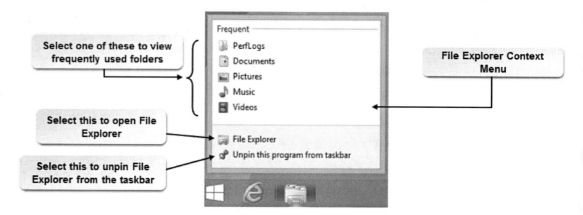

Figure 3-3: A context menu.

Dialog Boxes

A dialog box is a type of window that pops up, usually from within an application, and offers several options or instructions, prompting the user to respond. They are called dialog boxes because of this interaction or "dialog" between the computer and the user.

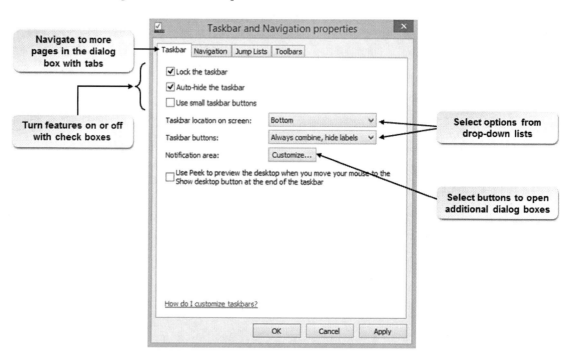

Figure 3-4: The Taskbar and Navigation Properties dialog box.

The following table lists some of the common elements found in dialog boxes.

Element	Description
Button	With buttons, you can accept any changes made and close out of dialog boxes, open new dialog boxes, and navigate to more pages in a dialog box through tabs.
Check box	Check boxes are used to turn a specific feature on or off, signified by a check mark inside of a box or an empty box, respectively.
Radio button	Radio buttons perform the same basic function as check boxes, but allow you to choose only one of a set of options. An activated radio button shows a filled circle, whereas unactivated radio buttons show an empty circle.
Text box	A text box allows you to enter text, usually a message or name, as a value.
Drop-down list	Selecting the arrow on a drop-down list expands a list of multiple options from which you can choose. Selecting the arrow again collapses the list.
Spin box	Spin boxes are usually up and down, or left and right arrows that allow you to increment or decrement values one at a time. For example, selecting the down arrow with a value of 5 will change the value to 4.

Desktop Icons

Desktop icons are small, labeled pictures that are displayed on the body of the Desktop. Like tiles on the **Start** screen, Desktop icons can act as shortcuts for running programs, and they can also represent individual files and folders that have been saved to the Desktop. Each icon is named and has a stylized picture associated with it. Unlike tiles, which you activate by clicking them once, Desktop icons are activated when you double-click them. You can make Desktop icons smaller or larger, and move and rearrange them to suit your needs. Desktop icon management options are available in the icon or Desktop context menus.

 Note: When Windows 8.1 is first loaded on your computer, one Desktop icon, **Recycle Bin**, appears. The next topic has details about the Recycle Bin.

 Access the Checklist tile on your LogicalCHOICE course screen for reference information and job aids on How to Navigate the Desktop.

ACTIVITY 3–1
Navigating Desktop Elements

Before You Begin
You are at the **Start** screen and the **Switcher** is closed.

Scenario
Because you're going to start using the Desktop often, you want to examine its basic elements: the **Notification** area, Desktop icons, and the taskbar, and determine how they can best work for you. In order to maximize your comfort level with your Desktop experience, you'll want to remove the clutter of **Notification** icons that you don't look at daily, but still want available. You see yourself using the taskbar quite a bit to launch apps, so you'll arrange it in a way that looks the most appealing and accessible. Lastly, you've realized that the majority of your work will be done with Desktop apps, so you decide to make your computer boot directly to the Desktop, bypassing the **Start** screen. This way, the **Start** screen will still be there, but only when you specifically call for it.

1. Explore the Desktop.
    a) On the **Start** screen, select the **Desktop** tile.
    b) Locate the **Recycle Bin** icon on the Desktop.

    c) Locate the taskbar along the bottom of the page.

    d) Place your pointer over each taskbar icon to view its tooltip description. The tooltips show the application names: Internet Explorer and File Explorer.

 Note: The **Start** button does not show a tooltip when you hover the pointer over it.

    e) Locate the icons in the **Notification** area and view their tooltips.

2. Hide notification items.
    a) In the **Notification** area, select the **Show hidden icons** up arrow.

b) Verify that the **hidden icons** menu appears.

c) From the **Notification** area, drag the **Action Center** icon up into the **hidden icons** menu.

> **Note:** If the **Show hidden icons** up arrow is not present, dragging an icon up from the taskbar will open the **hidden icons** menu.

d) Do the same for the **Speakers** and **Internet access** icons.

e) If necessary, select anywhere on the Desktop background to close the **hidden icons** menu.

3. Display the taskbar in alternate locations.
    a) Right-click the taskbar to open the taskbar context menu.
    b) Verify that **Lock the taskbar** is checked.

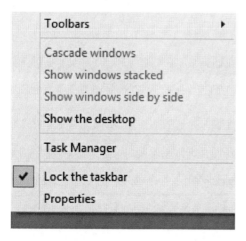

c) Select **Lock the taskbar** to uncheck this option. The context menu closes.
d) Open the taskbar context menu.
e) Verify that **Lock the taskbar** is no longer checked.
f) Select outside of the context menu to close it.
g) Drag the taskbar to the left, right, or top of the screen and then release.

Note: The taskbar can be moved and locked to any side you choose.

The taskbar is now displayed on that edge of the screen.

h) If you prefer, drag the taskbar back to the bottom of the screen.

i) Open the taskbar context menu and check **Lock the taskbar** to lock it.

4. Set the property that allows you to boot directly to the Desktop.

a) Open the taskbar context menu.

b) Select **Properties**. Verify that the **Taskbar and Navigation properties** dialog box opens.

c) Select the **Navigation** tab.

d) Under the **Start screen** section, check the **When I sign in or close all apps on a screen, go to the desktop instead of Start** check box.

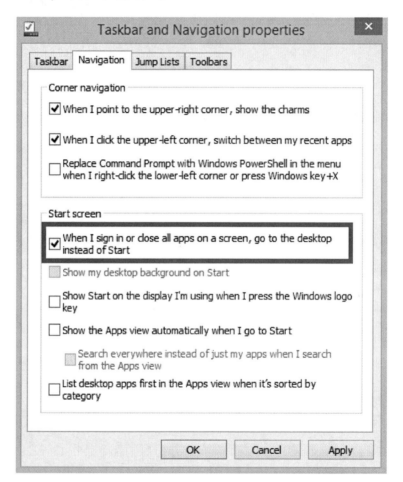

e) Select **OK** to confirm this change and close the dialog box.

TOPIC B

Manage Files and Folders with File Explorer

Now that you've become familiar with some of the elements of the Desktop, it's time to take a look at the organization and management of the products of your work: files and folders. Just as it is with paper files and folders, in order to keep track of your daily tasks, you'll need to organize the work you do on your computer. In this topic, you will explore how data is stored on your PC and how you can manage your files using the methods available on the Desktop.

Files and Folders

In your office, you work with paper files that you store within labeled folders in a file cabinet. If the files and folders are properly labeled and organized, it's easy to find what you're looking for. Computers work in a similar fashion, where the documents, reports, and other data you create in your applications are saved in files and stored in folders. When you are ready to save your work in an application, you assign a name to the file and select or create a folder in which to store it. The name you give to the file should be descriptive enough to help you find the file in the future.

Folders are the directories in which you store your files. As with a file cabinet, you can have folders within folders. For instance, on your computer, you might have a folder for all invoices for the current year. That might be the equivalent of a cabinet drawer. Within that, you might have a folder for each customer, labeled with the customer or company name. Within the customer folder would be all of the invoices, or files, for that customer. In this way, folders keep your files organized for easy access. The Desktop itself is a directory, and many people choose to save their files and folders to it. In this case, access is not only easy, but quick, as the Desktop is one of the first screens that you will see.

Libraries

Libraries look and act like folders, but are designed to be more like the card catalog. They don't actually store your files; instead, they keep track of file and folder locations so you don't have to, and present them in a single area. Libraries can even keep track of folders that are stored on different hard drives, removable storage (such as a flash drive or SD card), or even a different computer. Windows comes preloaded with four libraries: **Documents**, **Music**, **Pictures**, and **Videos**. Windows 8.1 provides the connectivity between programs and the libraries, so that word-processor program files are displayed in the **Documents** library, image files are displayed in the **Pictures** library, and so on. You can create new libraries if these four don't meet your needs.

File Explorer

Just as with a file cabinet, the files and folders on your PC occasionally need to be cleaned up and reorganized. *File Explorer* gives you a way of viewing and managing the filing system on your computer. By using File Explorer, you can rename, move, or copy any file or folder, as well as create new folders. You can even open files to work on. When you open a file from within File Explorer, the appropriate application is started and your file is opened within the application.

File Explorer runs in a directory window, which displays files, folders, and subfolders and contains several elements that are common to Desktop windows.

Figure 3-5: Elements of a File Explorer window.

Elements of a File Explorer Window

The following table lists the various elements of a File Explorer window and their functions.

Element	Function
Navigation pane	Shows you locations available on your computer (libraries, favorite or recently used locations, and storage drives), as well as other computers that may be networked to yours.
Contents pane	Displays the files and folders contained within the locations listed in the **Navigation** pane.
Tabs	Categories of tools used for managing your files. Each tab has an attached ribbon or menu of specialized tools. The tabs vary depending on the directory in which they appear, but most directories have **File** and **Home** tabs.
Ribbon	A menu of file-management tools related to the tab selected. The tools contained within the ribbon vary depending on the directory in which they appear.
Address bar	The **Address** bar shows you what folder you are in and the structure of the path from the file or folder up to the library or disk-drive level. You can select any of these levels to move up the structure.
Search bar	The **Search** bar allows you to search for files and folders within disk drives, libraries, and folders.
Back and **Forward** buttons	Use these to go to a previous page, or forward a page, respectively.
Up one level button	Use this button to move up a level within the file path structure.

Element	Function
Caret	Indicates that a library or folder contains subfolders. You select the caret to open the library or folder and display its contents, or to close the library or folder and hide the contents.

Tabs and the Ribbon

The *ribbon* is composed of tabs, groups, and commands for managing, editing, and viewing files. You can select each of the tabs along the top of the ribbon to access a specialized ribbon of tools related to that tab. Access functions on the ribbon by selecting the icons on the ribbon. Some icons will open drop-down menus or dialog boxes offering more options. Tabs and the contents of ribbons vary from directory to directory, although most have **File**, **Home**, and **View** tabs. You can expand or minimize the ribbon by using the caret at the right end of the **Tabs** bar.

 Note: This course uses a streamlined notation for ribbon commands. They'll appear as "**[Ribbon Tab]→[Group]→[Button or Control]**" as in "select **Home→Clipboard→Paste**." If the group name isn't needed for navigation or there isn't a group, it's omitted, as in "select **File→Open**."

Contextual Tabs

Contextual tabs are additional tabs that appear on the ribbon when you work with certain objects or functions. The commands and options available on these tabs are restricted to those particular functions. For example, the Recycle Bin has the **Recycle Bin Tools Manage** contextual tab, only available with the Recycle Bin. You can switch between the contextual tabs and the core tabs as needed.

The Recycle Bin

When you delete something from your computer, such as a data file or folder, Windows doesn't actually delete it, but moves it into the *Recycle Bin*. The file will remain in the Recycle Bin until you empty it, at which time all files in the Recycle Bin will be permanently deleted. You can go into the Recycle Bin and delete files individually, restore a file that was deleted, or empty the Recycle Bin. To access the Recycle Bin, double-click the **Recycle Bin** Desktop icon. If you look on the taskbar, you'll note that the Recycle Bin uses the File Explorer directory window in which to run. If you run both the Recycle Bin and File Explorer at the same time, the taskbar will show the overlapping File Explorer icon. The **Recycle Bin** Desktop icon changes as it fills up with deleted files. When it is empty, the basket icon looks empty. As it fills up, more "paper" appears in the basket.

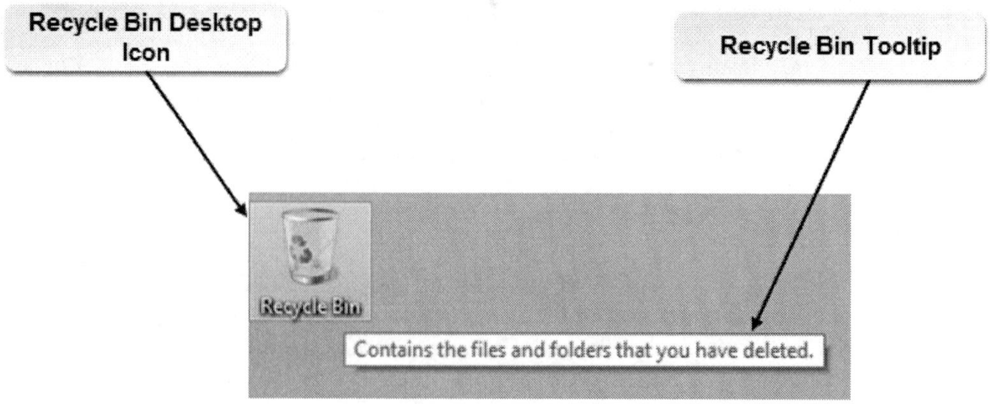

Recycle Bin Desktop Icon
Recycle Bin Tooltip
Recycle Bin
Contains the files and folders that you have deleted.

Figure 3-6: The Recycle Bin icon and tooltip.

	Access the Checklist tile on your LogicalCHOICE course screen for reference information and job aids on How to Manage Files and Folders.

ACTIVITY 3-2
Managing Files and Folders

Data Files

This PC\Documents\Mental Fitness_corrected.rtf

This PC\Documents\Working with Desktop Applications\Mental Fitness_draft.rtf

Scenario

You're the new editor of the Bit by Bit Fitness newsletter, and an author has submitted an article to you for editing. You've already made spelling and grammar corrections to the author's draft and saved it as a new, updated file. There are still more adjustments to make, however. Because you want to improve your productivity for future projects, you decide to start by moving the version you've started editing to a new location on the Desktop, where it will be more readily accessible. For the sake of being more organized, you then realize it will be better to send future works in progress to a specific folder on the Desktop, instead of just scattering them around. You still have the original draft that the author submitted, and as you no longer need it, you'll delete the file.

1. Open File Explorer.
   a) On the taskbar, select the **File Explorer** icon.

   b) Verify that File Explorer is open.

2. Find the newsletter article saved to your **Documents** folder.
   a) In the **Navigation** pane, select the caret next to **This PC**.
   b) Under **This PC**, select the **Documents** folder to view the contents of your local documents folder.

   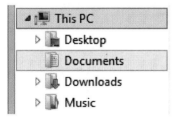

c) In the **Contents** pane, verify that there are two files: **Mental Fitness_corrected** and **Mental Fitness_draft**.

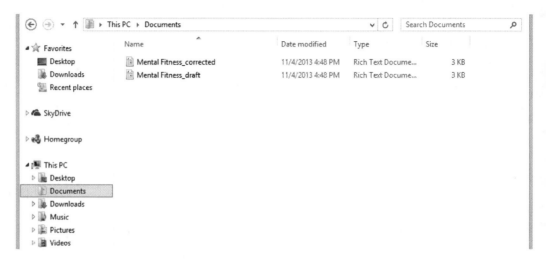

3. Copy a file.
   a) Select the file **Mental Fitness_corrected**.
   b) From the ribbon, select the **Home→Organize→Copy to**.

c) From the drop-down list, select **Desktop**.

d) Verify that **Documents** still contains the file **Mental Fitness_corrected**, and that there is a **Mental Fitness_corrected** file on the Desktop.

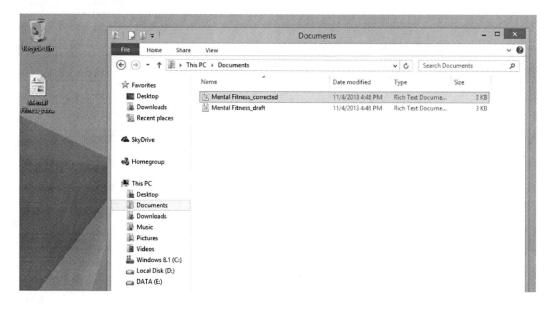

4. Create and name a new folder.
    a) From the **Navigation** pane of File Explorer, select the **Desktop** folder under **This PC**.

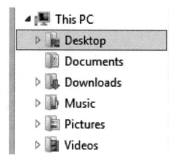

b) From the ribbon, select **Home→New→New folder**.

c) In the **New folder** text box, type *Works in progress* to name the folder.
d) Press the **Enter** key.

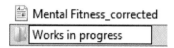

5. Move the file to the newly created folder.
   a) From the **Contents** pane of File Explorer, drag the file **Mental Fitness_corrected** into the **Works in progress** folder. When **Works in progress** is highlighted, release the file.

   b) From the **Contents** pane, open the **Works in progress** folder and verify that the **Mental Fitness_corrected** file is inside.
   c) If necessary, right-click the Desktop and select **Refresh** so that the Desktop reflects the changes you just made.

6. Delete the pre-edit draft file.
   a) From the **Navigation** pane, under **This PC**, select **Documents**.
   b) In the **Documents** folder, select the file **Mental Fitness_draft**.
   c) From the ribbon, select **Home→Organize→Delete**.
   d) Confirm that the file is deleted and no longer resides in the **Documents** folder.

7. View the contents of the Recycle Bin, and then empty the Recycle Bin.
   a) Double-click the **Recycle Bin** icon on the Desktop to open the Recycle Bin.
   b) Verify that the application opens.

 Note: The Recycle Bin uses the File Explorer directory window. Because both File Explorer and the Recycle Bin are open, there will be two File Explorer icons overlapping on the taskbar.

   c) From the ribbon, select **Recycle Bin Tools Manage→Manage→Empty Recycle Bin**.

d) In the **Delete File** dialog box, select **Yes**. The file is deleted and no longer appears in the **Contents** pane.

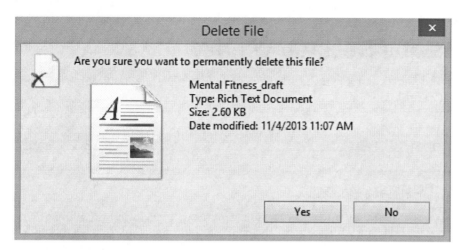

e) Leave the Recycle Bin and File Explorer windows open.

 Note: To further explore File Explorer navigation techniques, you can access the LearnTO **Customize File Explorer** presentation from the **LearnTO** tile on the LogicalCHOICE Course screen.

TOPIC C

Elements of a Desktop Window

As you saw with the File Explorer and Recycle Bin windows, all Desktop applications are designed to run within a standardized window using common elements. Once you become familiar with how the components of a window work, using new applications and switching between applications will be easier. In this topic, you'll identify more elements of a Desktop window and move, resize, and switch between windows.

Desktop Windows

When you run an application on the Desktop, it runs within a graphical window, with borders that you can drag to resize and change the shape of the window. Although you can have multiple windows open, only one window can be active at a time. To make it easy to identify the active window, the borders of the active window are colorful, whereas the borders of inactive windows are gray. There are three types of Desktop windows covered in this course: the directory window and the dialog box (which were discussed in previous topics), and the application window, which is explored in this topic.

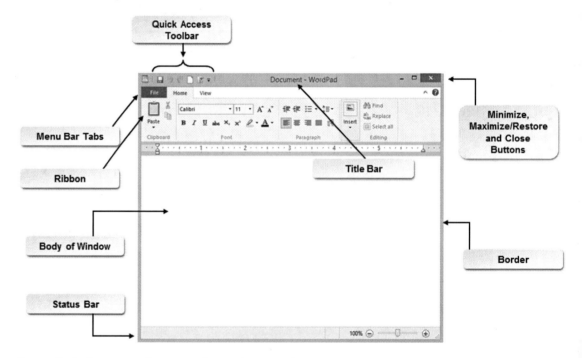

Figure 3-7: Common elements of a Desktop window.

Elements of a Desktop Window

The following table describes the elements of a Desktop window.

Window Element	Description
Border	In the **Restore** state, borders frame the window and can be used to change the size of the window. Dragging the sides makes the window wider or narrower; dragging the top or bottom makes it taller or shorter. Dragging a corner will adjust the width and height at the same time. An exception to this is the dialog box, which typically cannot be resized.
Title bar	At the top of the window, the title bar shows the name of the application or file you are using. You can use the title bar to drag the window, and to snap the application, just as you snap Windows Store apps.
Minimize button	This button lets you temporarily close the window, leaving the application running. The application's icon will remain on the taskbar and will be highlighted to indicate the application is still running.
Restore/Maximize button	These two share the same position on the title bar. The **Maximize** icon looks like a single window and the **Restore** icon looks like two windows cascading. **Maximize** resizes the window to fill the screen. No borders will be visible. **Restore** reduces the window to run in a smaller size, with visible borders. Most dialog boxes cannot be maximized.
Close button	Shuts down the application and closes the window.
Control menu	Gives you **Minimize, Maximize, Restore,** and **Close** options in menu form. May also have other options depending on the application.
Quick Access Toolbar	Provides icons for performing frequently used actions such as saving and printing. May also have other options depending on the application.
Status bar	The status bar is the area where the application displays information about items selected, what page you are on, if **Caps Lock** is on, and other messages that aid in use of the application. There is often a **Zoom** bar on the right side, which lets you increase or decrease the size of the page being viewed.

The Quick Access Toolbar

The **Quick Access Toolbar** displays icons that with one click can perform functions that otherwise might take several motions. In applications such as word processors and spreadsheets, this tiny area can be a huge time saver. To add a function to the **Quick Access Toolbar**, select the **Customize Quick Access Toolbar** icon to open the menu and select the function to be included on the display. Functions that are already displayed on the toolbar have a check next to them. To remove a function from the toolbar, select the check to remove it.

The following table lists options that are commonly found on the **Quick Access Toolbar**.

Figure 3-8: Typical Quick Access Toolbar menu customization options.

Icon	Function
Open	Opens an existing file.
New	Opens a blank page so you can create a new file.
Save	Saves the file using the current name and location. You can use this function the first time you save a new file, but you will be directed to the **Save As** dialog box.
Save As	Requires you to assign a name and location to the file before saving it. Use this when you wish to keep both the original file and the modified file, and the first time you save a new file.
Undo	Undoes the last action taken on the file. Some applications allow you to undo several actions.
Redo	Repeats the last action taken on the file. Can be used to reverse the last **Undo**.
Print	Sends the file to a printer or a print file. This option allows you to select a printer, select the pages to be printed, and adjust settings on the printer before sending the file to be printed.
Print Preview	Allows you to view the file on the screen as it would look if it were printed on a piece of paper.
Quick print	Allows you to print the file without having to select a printer or print options. It uses the same settings as the most recently printed file.

The Body of the Window

The *body* of the window is where your work is displayed. It takes on a different appearance depending on the application. In a directory window, the body is composed of the **Navigation** pane and the **Contents** pane. In a word-processing application, the body of the window is where you type; it looks like a piece of paper with rulers along the top or left. In a spreadsheet, the body is a grid pattern composed of rows and columns of cells in which you do your work.

Snap, Cascade, Stack, and Switch Functions

As with apps, you can switch between windows, and snap them to view more than one at a time. Desktop windows can also be cascaded and stacked on top of each other, and you can have more than two windows showing at once. You can snap windows by using the title bar to drag the window, but cascade and stack are available only by opening the taskbar context menu.

 Access the Checklist tile on your LogicalCHOICE course screen for reference information and job aids on How to Use the Elements of a Desktop Window.

ACTIVITY 3-3
Working with the Elements of a Desktop Window

Before You Begin
File Explorer and the Recycle Bin are open and in the **Restore** state.

Scenario
Now that you know how to manage files and folders, and have worked with directory windows and dialog boxes, you want to focus on where the real work takes place on the Desktop: within application windows. You'll clean your virtual workspace by closing the Recycle Bin you no longer need to look at, and to start multitasking on the Desktop, you'll open a new WordPad application window side-by-side with File Explorer. In order to get the two windows just the way you want them to appear, you'll arrange them in a variety of ways until you find what you're most comfortable with. You also decide to customize the **Quick Access Toolbar** in WordPad to add commands you plan on using often.

---

1. Close the Recycle Bin window.
   a) On the title bar of the Recycle Bin window, locate the **Close** button.
   b) Select the **Close** button to close the Recycle Bin.

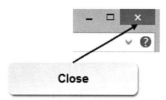

   c) Verify that the **Documents** File Explorer window is now the active window.

2. Move the File Explorer window to get a better view.
   a) Place the pointer on the File Explorer title bar and drag the window around on the page.
   b) Release the title bar when it's at a position you prefer. The window will stay where you put it.

    Caution: The title bar has two move functions. For moving the window, the pointer should retain its normal shape. For resizing the border by dragging the window, the pointer should look like a two-headed arrow.

3. Resize the File Explorer window to your preference.
   a) Place your pointer over the right border of the window. The pointer becomes a two-headed arrow.
   ⟺
   b) Drag the border to the right until the window's width is to your liking.
   c) Place your pointer on the top edge of the title bar until it becomes a two-headed arrow. ↕
   d) Drag the top border up until the window's height is to your liking.

4. Maximize the File Explorer window to get a full view.

a) On the title bar, locate the **Maximize** button.

b) Select the **Maximize** button to enlarge the window.
    The window fills the screen, and you cannot see the window borders.

5. Minimize the File Explorer window.
    a) Select the **Minimize** button.

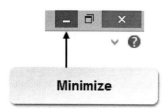

The window closes, but you can see on the taskbar that the **File Explorer** icon is highlighted, indicating that the application is still running.
    b) On the taskbar, select the **File Explorer** icon to maximize the window again.

6. Snap the File Explorer window to the right side of the screen.
    a) Use the title bar to drag the File Explorer window off the right side of the screen.
    b) When you see a small visual "wave" around your pointer, release the window.

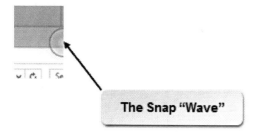

The window snaps to fill the right side of the screen.
    c) Verify that you can see the Desktop on the left side of your screen.

7. Open WordPad.
    a) Using the **Search Charm**, type *WordPad* into the search box.

b) From the search results, select **WordPad**.

c) On the Desktop, verify that File Explorer is still snapped and WordPad is in the **Restore** state. WordPad is the active window.

8. Snap WordPad to the left side of the Desktop.

a) Use the title bar to drag the WordPad window off the left side of the screen.

b) Release the window when you see the small wave.
You now have two applications displayed on the screen. WordPad is still the active window

9. Arrange the windows in a variety of ways.

a) Right-click the taskbar to open the context menu.

b) Select **Cascade windows**.

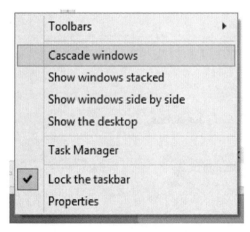

The windows cascade down from the upper-left corner.

c) Open the context menu again and select **Show windows stacked**.
The windows rearrange horizontally, with the active window on the top.

d) Open the context menu again and select **Show windows side by side**.
The windows are put back in the snapped position.
e) Close File Explorer.
f) In the WordPad window, select the **Maximize** button to maximize WordPad.

10. Add icons to the WordPad **Quick Access Toolbar**.

a) At the top left of the title bar, select the **Customize Quick Access Toolbar** icon ▾ to open the menu.

b) Select **New**.
c) Verify that the **Quick Access Toolbar** now has an icon of a blank sheet of paper. This icon will open a new, blank document.

d) Open the **Customize Quick Access Toolbar** menu again.
e) Confirm that **New** now has a check next to it, signifying that it is available on the toolbar.
f) From the menu, select **Open**.
g) Verify that the toolbar now has an icon of a folder with an arrow pointing into it.

TOPIC D

Create and Modify Files with Desktop Applications

Windows 8.1 comes bundled with a few simple but useful applications. You've already used File Explorer and Recycle Bin, and have opened WordPad. WordPad is one of many Desktop apps that allows you create and edit individual files in a number of ways. Using features common to these apps will provide you with greater control over the content of your files, and you'll be able to apply these features to many other apps you're likely to use in your day-to-day work.

New Documents

When you open an application, whether it is a word processor, spreadsheet, or graphics program, the work area is blank and ready for you to create a new document. However, there will be times when you are working on a document and wish to have a blank slate to create a new document. To do this, you can select the **New** command on the **File** tab of the ribbon. If you have customized your **Quick Access Toolbar** to include it, you can select the **New** icon and it will do the same thing. Some applications, such as WordPad and Notepad, will not let you have more than one document open at a time and will close the file you are currently working on when you open a second file. When this happens, the application will ask if you want to save your work on the current file before it is closed. New documents often start with a generic name that is displayed in the title bar. For example, word processing apps such as WordPad will display "Document" in the title bar until you give the document a name.

Existing Documents

It's often useful to be able to modify existing files. You may have a spreadsheet that needs correcting or updating; or you may find that reusing a document and making a few small changes can save time. From the **File** tab menu, when you select **Open** (or select the **Quick Access Toolbar's Open** icon), a dialog box will open, allowing you to search through your folders to find the file you wish to use. Select the file and select **Open**, and your file will be opened for use. You can make any changes you wish, but no changes will be permanent until you save the file with the changes.

Save

When you are finished working on a file, or you have reached a point at which you don't want to lose your work, you can save the file. When you make changes to an existing file, you can save it under the current name, which will overwrite the previous version of the file, or you can use **Save as** to give it a new name. This will give you a new file and will leave the original file as it was. The first time you save a new file, you will be asked to name it and choose a folder to save it in. File names can include letters, numbers, spaces, and some special characters. Names cannot contain the following symbols: < > . : " / \ | ? *. Both **Save** and **Save as** are available on the **File** tab of the ribbon. The **Save** function is also available on the **Quick Access Toolbar** and its icon looks like a small blue storage disk.

 Note: Saving often while working on a file is advisable. If your computer loses power or has technical trouble, you can lose all of your work. If you save frequently, you'll lose only the work you have done since the last save.

The Clipboard

The *Clipboard* enables you to move text or graphics within your document and between applications. The following table lists the various functions of the Clipboard.

Clipboard Function	Used To
Cut	Remove the selected item from its original location and place it on the Clipboard. This is similar to File Explorer's **Move to** function.
Copy	Keep the selected item in its original location and also place it on the Clipboard. This is similar to File Explorer's **Copy to** function.
Paste	Place Clipboard items (cut or copied) into a new location. The contents of the Clipboard remain there until you replace them with another selection, lock or sign out of your account, or turn off your PC. This allows you to paste the same item over and over again.
Paste special	Paste items in a special format of your choosing. For example, you can select **Unformatted Text** from the **Paste Special** dialog box to remove any bolding or coloring in the text you copied to the Clipboard.

Undo and Redo

The beauty of a word-processing program is that you can quickly correct mistakes. As you saw earlier, the **Backspace** key on your keyboard will undo a mistake in typing. But **Backspace** won't work when you make other mistakes, like accidentally cutting or pasting the wrong area, or typing over text. **Undo** and **Redo**, located on the **Quick Access Toolbar**, can help. **Undo** looks like a small arrow pointing to the left and will undo your last action. **Redo** will repeat your last action, or redo something that you just undid. Some word-processing applications allow you to undo and redo several actions, and often there is a drop-down menu for the **Undo** icon, which enables you to undo several actions at once.

Print

When you are ready to commit your document to paper, you can use the **Print** function. **Print** offers several options for printing: you can print the entire document, a range of pages, the current page, or a selected part of the document. You can send the print request to a printer and have your document printed on paper, or send it to a print file for use later or to share with others. There are three print functions:

- **Print** gives you the opportunity to make some choices when printing, such as selecting the printer, the number of copies to be printed, and which pages to print.
- **Quick print** will use the default printer and print the entire document, eliminating the need to go through the steps of making those choices.
- **Print preview** lets you view your file on the screen to see if it looks like you want it to before you print it. This eliminates running back and forth to the printer and wasting paper as you try to get the document to look just right.

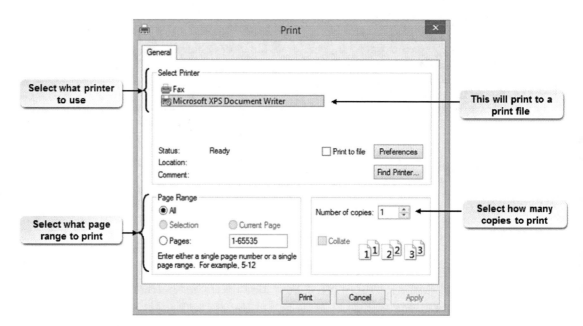

Figure 3-9: The Print dialog box.

 Access the Checklist tile on your LogicalCHOICE course screen for reference information and job aids on How to Create and Modify Files Using a Desktop Application.

ACTIVITY 3-4
Creating and Modifying Files with WordPad

Data Files

This PC\Desktop\Works in progress\Mental Fitness_corrected.rtf

Before You Begin

File Explorer is closed and WordPad is maximized on your screen.

Scenario

Although you've done a first edit on the author's **Mental Fitness** document, you need to implement some more stylistic changes. You'll open the document and replace some words. While making these changes, you slip up and need to undo your mistake. When you're done, you'll save the updated document and give it a new name. All of these actions are relatively quick and easy to perform, and they'll save you a great deal of time when you work in many other Desktop apps.

1. Open the **Mental Fitness_corrected** document.
   a) On the **Quick Access Toolbar**, select the **Open** icon.

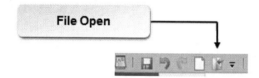

 Note: The **Open** command is also available on the **File** tab of the ribbon.

   b) In the **Open** dialog box, in the **Navigation** pane, under **This PC**, select **Desktop**.
   c) In the **Contents** pane, open the **Works in progress** folder and select the **Mental Fitness_corrected** file.

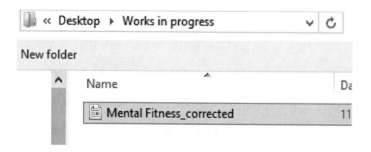

   d) Select the **Open** button to open the file.

2. Replace text.
   a) Use the pointer to double-click the word "push" in the first paragraph to select it.

The push for more physical education

b) Type the word **call** so that the word "push" is replaced with "call".

The call for more physical education

3. Remove multiple words.
   a) Use the pointer to drag over the words "it seems that" in the second paragraph to select them.

The findings of a recent study conducted by a university in Finland concluded that there was a strong correlation between poor academic performance, especially in reading and math skills, and poor motor skills. Children who struggled in the areas of agility, dexterity, and speed likewise tended to score lower on written tests. This may not be definitive proof, as correlation doesn't always imply causation, but it seems that even if poor motor skills didn't cause these children to suffer academically, they likely made their situation worse.

b) Press the **Delete** key.

but even if poor motor skills didn't cause these

4. To undo the deletion, on the **Quick Access Toolbar**, select **Undo** to return the words "it seems that" to the document.

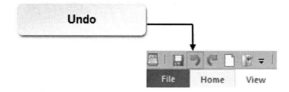

5. Remove the correct word.
   a) Select anywhere outside the highlighted text to deselect it.
   b) Highlight the word "that" in the same sentence and press **Delete**.
   c) Verify that the sentence reads "...but it seems even if poor motor skills..."

but it seems even if poor motor skills

6. Use the Clipboard to copy and paste text.
   a) If necessary, scroll down, and from the fourth paragraph, highlight the words "Bit by Bit Fitness is".

This is why Bit by Bit Fitness is expanding its programming to include a sort of extracurricular physical education for children who don't get enough at school or at home. Rest assured that this new program is far from being intense or excessive. The activities we have planned are no more strenuous than what a child would normally see at school or on a playground. Likewise, our aim is not only provide children with a safe environment that will benefit their physical health, but to provide activities that are actually fun and take away the stigma of exercise.

b) From the ribbon, select **Home→Clipboard→Copy** to copy the words "Bit by Bit Fitness is" to the Clipboard.

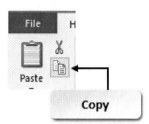

c) In the last paragraph, highlight the word "we're".

Our new program will start on Monday, January 13th -- we're excited to reveal more specifics as the weeks go by, so stay tuned!

d) From the ribbon, select **Home→Clipboard→Paste** to replace "we're" with the contents of the Clipboard.

 Note: Make sure to select the **Paste** button (represented by the Clipboard) and not its down arrow.

7. Save the file in the **Works in progress** folder.
   a) From the ribbon, select **File→Save as**.

b) In the **Save As** dialog box, in the **File name** text box, verify that the word **Mental Fitness_corrected** is showing and is highlighted.

File name: Mental Fitness_corrected

c) In the **File name** text box, type *Mental Fitness_revised* to rename the document.

File name: | Mental Fitness_revised

d) On the **Address** bar, verify that the **Works in progress** folder is the destination folder.

e) Select the **Save** button.
The file is saved, the **Save As** dialog box closes, and you are returned to your document.

f) On the title bar, confirm the file name **Mental Fitness_revised** has replaced **Mental Fitness_corrected**.

Mental Fitness_revised - WordPad

8. Leave the document open.

ACTIVITY 3-5
Printing a Document

Before You Begin
Mental Fitness_revised is still open.

Scenario
You're finished making changes to the article for now, and you'd like to be able mark up a hard copy. By using **Print preview**, you'll see how the document will look on the page before you print it. Then you'll open the **Page Setup** dialog box and remove page numbers before finally printing the document.

1. Preview the document.
   a) From the ribbon, select **File→Print→Print preview**.

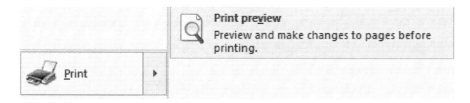

   b) Preview the document.
   c) Select anywhere on the page to zoom in on the page.
   d) Identify the groups and commands on the **Print preview** tab of the ribbon.
   e) From the ribbon, select **Print preview→Print→Page setup**.

   f) If necessary, in the **Page Setup** dialog box, uncheck the **Print Page Numbers** check box.

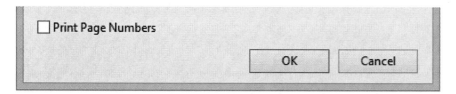

   g) Select **OK**.

h) From the ribbon, select **Print preview→Close→Close print preview** to go back to your document.

2. Print the document.
   a) From the ribbon, select **File→Print** to open the **Print** dialog box.
   b) Identify the options available in the **Print** dialog box.
   c) In the **Select Printer** section, select the printer you wish to use. If your PC is not connected to a printer, use Microsoft XPS Document Writer to send the document to a print file.
   d) In the **Page Range** section, verify that **All** is selected to print the entire document.
   e) Select **Print** to begin printing. You may have to assign a file name and location if you are printing to a print file.

3. Close WordPad.

4. Return to the **Start** screen.

Summary

In this lesson, you identified the elements of the Desktop and a typical Desktop application window. You used an application to create and edit files; and saved, printed, and managed files and folders to help keep them organized. With this knowledge, you'll be able to create, modify, and organize documents and files at your office and at home.

What are some advantages to using applications on the Desktop?

What are the advantages to being able to create folders within folders? Are there disadvantages to having folders within folders?

 Note: Check your LogicalCHOICE Course screen for opportunities to interact with your classmates, peers, and the larger LogicalCHOICE online community about the topics covered in this course or other topics you are interested in. From the Course screen you can also access available resources for a more continuous learning experience.

4 | Using Internet Explorer 11

Lesson Time: 1 hour, 20 minutes

Lesson Objectives

In this lesson, you will use Internet Explorer 11. You will:

- Open Internet Explorer 11 and identify what a browser is.

- Set preferences and navigate the environment.

- Navigate Internet Explorer on the Desktop and change settings.

Lesson Introduction

In the "Using Windows Store Apps and Navigation Features" lesson, you used the Weather app to look at weather for different cities. Although the Weather app uses the Internet to gather information for many cities, the app is limited to showing only weather. To really be able to use the power of the Internet, you need to use an app like Internet Explorer® 11. It is bundled with Microsoft® Windows® 8.1 and ready for you to use.

TOPIC A

Navigate Internet Explorer 11

In today's workplace, it's imperative to be able to use the Internet to gather information, send email messages, and network with colleagues. Much of what you've learned about using Windows Store apps and Desktop applications will help you when using Internet Explorer 11.

Web Browsers and Search Engines

The words "Internet" and "World Wide Web" or "the web" are often used interchangeably, but they are not the same. The Internet is a system of interconnected networks of computers, which can be used for many things. The web is one particular use—a collection of documents and other resources that are accessed using the Internet. A *web browser* is a computer program that locates and displays information found on the web. Microsoft® Internet Explorer, Mozilla® Firefox®, Google Chrome™, and Apple® Safari® are examples of web browsers. A *search engine* is software that searches the web based on the search terms that you enter into it and returns a list of content that is relevant to these terms. Microsoft® Bing® and Google are both examples of search engines.

Internet Explorer 11

Internet Explorer 11 is a graphical web browser that comes bundled with Windows 8.1. With it, you can search the web for news, documents, images, and more. When you do a search with Internet Explorer 11, it sends your search request to Bing, Microsoft's search engine, which searches for websites, documents, and other resources that either contain that text, or are related to it in some way. Bing then sends the results back to Internet Explorer, where they are sorted and presented on your screen, with the more relevant or popular results listed first. You can also run Internet Explorer in a Desktop window—access it by selecting the **Internet Explorer** icon on the taskbar. Internet Explorer 11's default page is MSN, which is Microsoft's Internet portal. An *Internet portal* is a website that gathers information from many sources and presents it with a consistent look and feel on one website.

Figure 4-1: The Internet Explorer home page.

Note: To further explore using both versions of Internet Explorer in Windows 8.1, you can access the LearnTO **Choose How Windows 8.1 Launches Internet Explorer** presentation from the **LearnTO** tile on the LogicalCHOICE Course screen.

URLs

Everything on the Internet has a unique *Uniform Resource Locator (URL)*, which is also known as an address. If you know the address of the website you are looking for, you can enter it in the **Address** bar, and Internet Explorer 11 will retrieve that specific page and display it on your screen.

Bing

Accessible from Internet Explorer, the Bing home page displays a picture that changes every day. Three icons at the lower-right corner of the picture allow you to look at previous pictures, or search for information on the picture shown. As you move the pointer around the page, small squares called hotspots appear. When you hold the pointer over a hotspot, a tidbit of information related to the picture appears, along with a hyperlink (or link), which, when selected, will take you to another website or open up additional information on the current page. Whenever your pointer turns into a pointing hand, it indicates a link.

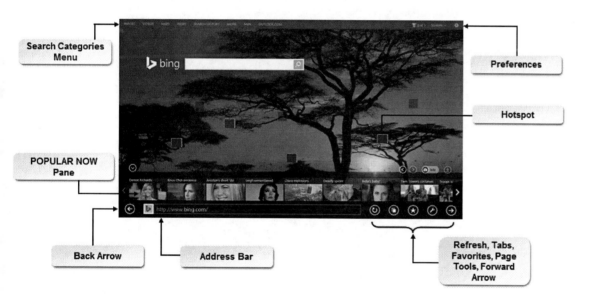

Figure 4-2: The Bing home page.

POPULAR NOW Pane

Above the bottom command bar on the Bing home page is the **POPULAR NOW** pane, which shows stories that are either currently in the news or have recently been searched for by many people. Small pictures called thumbnails, when selected, link to Bing searches using search terms related to the news item.

Search Categories Menu

Along the top of the Internet Explorer default page and the Bing home page are links to **OUTLOOK.COM**, Microsoft's email app, and **MSN**, along with search categories such as **IMAGES**, **VIDEOS**, **MAPS**, **NEWS**, and **SEARCH HISTORY**. Each search category comes with a drop-down menu offering more specific search options for that category. A larger list of categories is accessible under **MORE**.

 Access the Checklist tile on your LogicalCHOICE course screen for reference information and job aids on How to Navigate Internet Explorer 11 and Bing.

ACTIVITY 4-1
Navigating Internet Explorer 11

Before You Begin
You are viewing the **Start** screen.

Scenario
Because it is part of your job to keep abreast of trends in the news, being able to access the Internet is going to be invaluable. Before you can make full use of Internet Explorer, you need to know how to navigate around in it. You decide to visit several different news sources to get a well-rounded picture of the day's happenings. Once you have mastered these skills, you'll be able to use them in your leisure time as well at work.

1. Open Internet Explorer.
   a) Select the Internet Explorer tile.

   b) Verify that you are taken to the MSN home page. This is the default home page for Internet Explorer 11.

   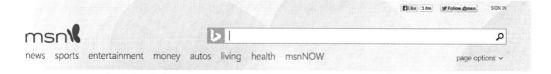

    Note: The MSN website changes frequently and may look slightly different than it does in the screenshots in this course.

2. Navigate using links.
   a) At the top of the page, under the MSN logo, select **news**.
   b) From the **msn news** page, verify that the topics on the page offer options related to news.
   c) From the options listed under the **msn news** logo, select **world** to navigate to a new page offering stories from around the world.

3. Navigate the page.
   a) Move the pointer over the page to identify the links available. Your pointer will look like a pointing hand when it is over a link.
   b) If necessary, use the scroll bar on the right side of the screen to view more of the page.

4. Navigate between pages.

a) Move the pointer to the center of the left side of the screen to reveal the **Back** arrow.

b) Select the arrow to return to the previous page.

5. Navigate to the Google home page.
   a) In the **Address** bar at the bottom, type *google.com*
   b) From the **Suggestions** menu, select **Google - www.google.com**.

c) From the top-right portion of the Google home page, select the **Apps** button.

d) From the drop-down list, select **News**.
   e) Verify that you are taken to a page that lists various news articles separated by category.
   f) Move your pointer to the right side of the page and use the scroll bar to scroll down the page and view more articles.
   g) Verify that the **Navigation** pane on the left stays in a fixed location when you scroll.

h) From the **Navigation** pane, select the **Technology** link.

Top Stories

    Mohamed Morsi

    Transportation Security
    Administration

    Philadelphia Eagles

    iPad

    BlackBerry Ltd

    Houston Texans

    Miami Dolphins

    YouTube

    Denver Broncos

    Rob Ford

Brighton, New York

World

U.S.

Business

Technology

Entertainment

Sports

Science

Health

Spotlight

You are taken to a page that lists articles exclusive to technology news.

6. Navigate to the Bing home page.
   a) If necessary, right-click anywhere on the page to bring up the bottom command bar.
   b) In the **Address** bar, type *Bing.com* and press **Enter**.

 Note: Because the picture changes every day, the pictures and links in the examples provided may not match the picture on your screen.

   c) Verify that the screen has icons—small images—and words in various sections.
   d) Move the pointer over the screen to activate the hotspots.
   e) Place the pointer over a hotspot to reveal a pane with information and an underlined link.

f) Move the pointer over the link within the **Information** pane.

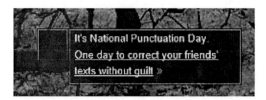

g) In the **Information** pane, select the link to begin the search.
h) Verify that the results on the new page are related to the link you selected.
i) Select the **Back** arrow to go back to the previous page.

7. Navigate using a categories menu.
    a) Identify the menu bar along the top of the Bing.com page.

b) Place your pointer over **NEWS** to open the drop-down menu.

c) Select **Get business news**.
d) Verify that the search returns news items relevant to the business world.

8. Use the **Back** arrow to return to the Bing home page.

TOPIC B

Browse the Web

You've seen how to move around and use the search links provided on the MSN and Bing pages, but the real power of the Internet is being able to specify your own search criteria. In your work, having the resources of the Internet at your fingertips will be invaluable.

The Search Bar

The **Search** bar is the text box located at the top or near the top of certain web pages. To perform a search, you enter a word or phrase into the **Search** bar text box, and the search engine scans for websites, documents, and other resources that have that word or phrase, or are related to it. The search engine then returns the results for your browser to display. The more specific your query, the better your results will be.

Search Suggestions

To use search suggestions, just begin typing in the **Search** bar. As you type, Internet Explorer tries to predict what you are looking for and offers a list of suggestions based on what you've typed, previous searches you have done, and similar searches that it has found on the Internet. If the list includes the term you intended to type into the **Search** bar text box, you can save time by selecting the suggestion to begin your search. Search suggestions can be turned on and off from the **Preferences** menu, which is discussed later in this topic.

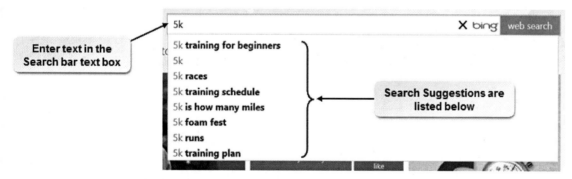

Figure 4–3: Search suggestions in Internet Explorer.

 Access the Checklist tile on your LogicalCHOICE course screen for reference information and job aids on How to Use the Search Bar.

The Command Bar

As with the other apps provided by Windows 8.1, Internet Explorer 11 has a hidden command bar. When you first open the app, the command bar along the bottom of the screen is visible, but will disappear when you select anything on the page. When you need to use it again, simply right-click the background of the screen to bring it back.

 Note: Right-clicking also opens the **Tabs** menu above the command bar. This menu is discussed later in the topic.

Internet Explorer 11 can be configured to always show the address bar and tabs. If the command bar remains open when you select something on the page, then this option has been configured.

The following table describes the elements of the Internet Explorer 11 command bar.

Element	Action
Address bar	Shows the address of the page you're on, and allows you to enter a specific website address to navigate to that site.
Back arrow	Located on the left side of the command bar, the **Back** arrow takes you back to the previous page.
Forward arrow	Located on the right side of the command bar, the **Forward** arrow takes you forward a page. **Forward** and **Back** take you only to pages you have viewed in the current session.
Refresh icon	Tells your computer to reload the page you're on. This can be helpful when the browser is running slowly, or on pages where information is fluid and may be updated in real time.
Tabs icon	Opens the **Tabs** menu. From here, you can navigate to and remain on multiple websites at one time.
Favorites icon	Opens the **Favorites** menu. From here, you can add a site to your favorites, select any site you've already added to your favorites, and pin a site to your **Start** screen.
Page tools icon	Enables you to search for text on the current page, view Internet Explorer 11 in a Desktop window, or view files you have downloaded.

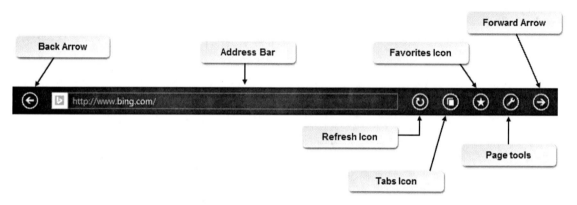

Figure 4–4: The Internet Explorer command bar.

 Access the Checklist tile on your LogicalCHOICE course screen for reference information and job aids on How to Use Icons on the Command Bar.

The Favorites Menu

Selecting the **Favorites** icon on the command bar will display the **Favorites** menu, which keeps a list of the websites you specifically choose to mark. From this menu, you can add websites to your list of favorites, pin tiles of those websites to your **Start** screen, and open the **Share Charm** to share your favorites with others. Selecting a favorites link will take you directly to the site listed on the link. Favorites links can also be grouped by custom-defined categories for easier management. The **Favorites** menu is available at all times when in Internet Explorer.

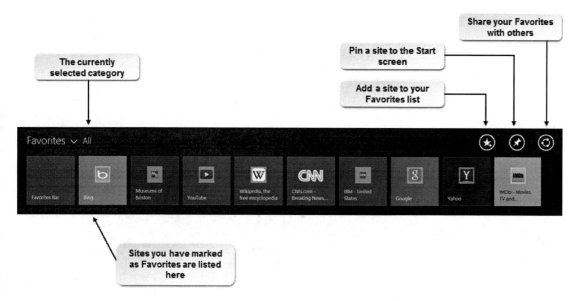

Figure 4-5: The Favorites menu.

The Frequent Menu

Selecting the **Address** bar will display the **Frequent** menu, which displays links to sites that you visit frequently. Selecting one of these links will take you directly to the site listed on the link. This menu is also available at all times when in Internet Explorer.

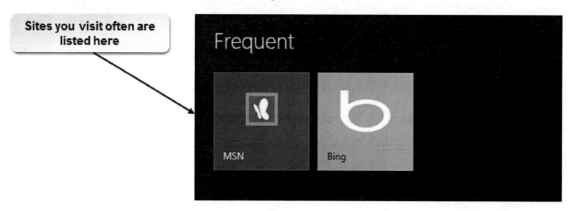

Figure 4-6: The Frequent menu.

 Access the **Checklist** tile on your **LogicalCHOICE** course screen for reference information and job aids on How to Use the Frequent Menu and the Favorites Menu.

The Tabs Menu

Internet Explorer lets you use more than one page at a time by using tabs. This allows you to do more than one search at a time and keeps the history of each search separate. You can open and manage tabs by using the **Tabs** menu. This menu shows what tabs are open and which tab you are currently using, and provides a means of switching between tabs. There is always one tab open during your browsing session, and you can have an unlimited number of tabs open at once. Each tab has a **Close** icon for closing it individually.

Also on the menu are the **New tab** and **Tab tools** icons. The **New tab** icon will open a new tab, while the **Tab tools** icon provides a menu where you can either reopen a closed tab or open an

InPrivate tab. Using an **InPrivate** tab temporarily prevents Internet Explorer from storing data about the browsing session for that tab. This is useful for when you are using a public or shared PC, and you don't want other users to be able to track the exact websites you browsed after you're done.

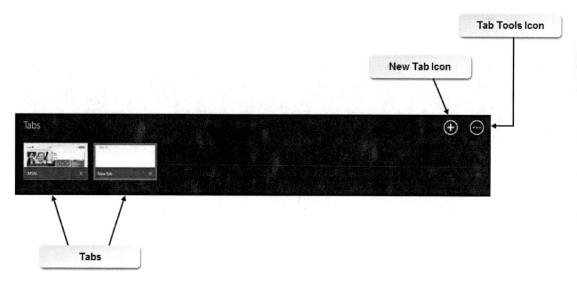

Figure 4-7: The Tabs menu.

 Access the Checklist tile on your LogicalCHOICE course screen for reference information and job aids on How to Use Tabs.

Bing Preferences

On the Bing website, the small gear at the top-right of your screen provides a link to your preferences. Preferences allow you to change settings that affect how you use Bing, such as filtering out unsafe text, images, and videos from your search results; allowing your browser to make suggestions based on your location or the text you type into the Bing **Search** box; and what language to use when displaying results. You can also turn the search history for Bing on or off, and view or clear your search history.

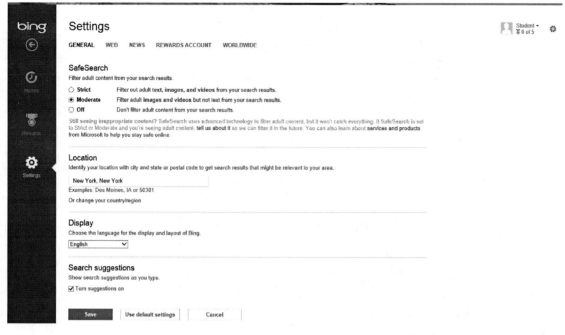

Figure 4-8: The Settings page of Bing Preferences.

 Note: To further explore search history on the Bing **Preferences** menu, you can access the LearnTO **Manage Your Online Search History** presentation from the **LearnTO** tile on the LogicalCHOICE Course screen.

 Access the Checklist tile on your LogicalCHOICE course screen for reference information and job aids on How to Set Bing Search Preferences.

The Share Charm

Using the **Share Charm**, you can quickly share the address or content of a website; pictures from your photo gallery; or content from an app with your Mail contacts. In addition to sharing content with Mail contacts, you can share with people in your social networks or add the item to your **Reading List** so you can review it at a later time. The **Share Charm** works with Windows 8.1 apps that support the function, but is limited to sharing screenshots with Desktop applications. To see if the **Share** feature works with the app you are using, from the **Charms** menu, select the **Share Charm**. The **Share** icon is also available on the **Favorites** menu in Internet Explorer.

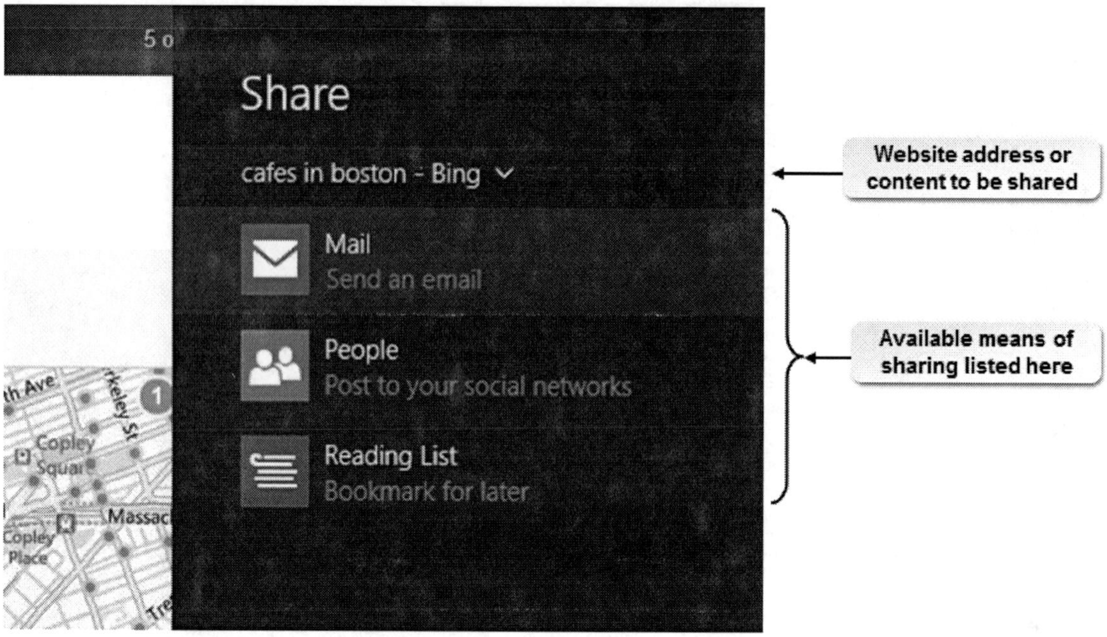

Share

cafes in boston - Bing ⌄

→ **Website address or content to be shared**

✉ Mail
Send an email

👥 People
Post to your social networks

≡ Reading List
Bookmark for later

→ **Available means of sharing listed here**

Figure 4-9: Sharing in Internet Explorer.

 Access the Checklist tile on your LogicalCHOICE course screen for reference information and job aids on How to Share.

ACTIVITY 4–2
Using Internet Explorer and Share

Before You Begin
You are at the Bing home page on Internet Explorer.

Scenario
On your upcoming business trip to Boston, you'd like to visit a museum and have lunch at a café with a colleague. In preparation, you'll search online for museums in the Boston area and save a museum site as a favorite. This will enable you to return to the site without having to search again. Keeping the search results handy, you'll open a second tab to conduct a search of Boston's cafés. Finally, you'll share the list of cafés you find with your colleague so she can help in choosing where to go.

---

1. Conduct a search.
   a) In the **Search** bar on the Bing home page, type *Boston museums*
   b) Verify that the suggestions listed change to fit your search terms as you type.
   c) From the suggestion list, select **boston museums**.

   d) Verify that there are several links listed that will take you to different websites on Boston museums.
   e) In the **Search** bar, confirm that your search term is still listed.

2. Redefine the search.
   a) In the search box, type a space, add the word *maps* to your search term, and press **Enter** to begin another search.

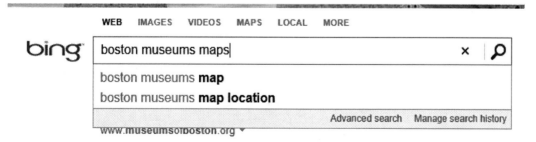

   b) Verify that the new search results provide links to sites with maps of Boston's museums.

c) Select **Museums of Boston** to go to that website.

WEB   IMAGES   VIDEOS   MAPS   NEWS   MORE

bing   boston museums maps

ALSO TRY: Top Museums in Boston · List of Museums in Boston · Car Museum B...

47,500,000 RESULTS   Any time ▼

Museums in **Boston**, Massachusetts | MapQuest
www.**mapquest**.com/**maps**?cat=**Museums**&city=**Boston**&state=MA ▼
Find **Museums** in **Boston**, Massachusetts provided by MapQuest. Find **Museums** locations in your local area - **maps**, directions, and phone numbers. View local ...

Museums of **Boston**
www.**museums**ofboston.org/index.php ▼
A collaboration of 40 Greater **Boston museums** of art, culture, history, nature and science, showcasing the cultural attractions of eastern Massachusetts.

3. Pin the site as a favorite.
   a) On the command bar, select the **Favorites** icon.

   b) From the **Favorites** menu, select **Add to favorites**.

c) Confirm that the title of the site is listed in the dialog box, and select **Add**. This site is now listed as one of your favorites.

4. View the **Favorites** menu.

a) Verify that the museum website is listed under the **Favorites** title.

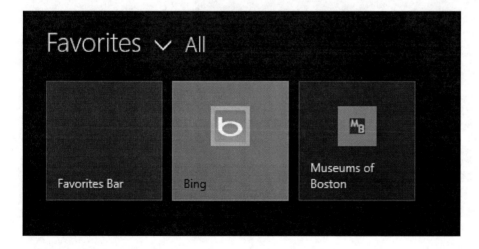

b) Select the background of the website page to close the **Favorites** menu and command bar.

5. Open a second tab and perform a search.

a) Right-click the background area of the page to open the **Tabs** menu.

b) Select the **New tab** icon to open a new tab.

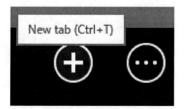

c) Verify that the page is blank and the **Frequent** menu is displayed.

d) In the **Search** bar text box at the bottom of the page, type *cafes in boston*

e) Above the **Search** text box, verify that suggestions are listed.

f) Select the **Go** icon 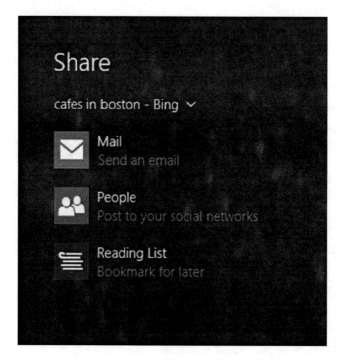 or press **Enter** to begin your search.

g) Confirm that the results of your search are presented on the page.

6. Share a link to a web page.

a) From the **Charms** menu, select **Share**.

b) From the list of apps, select **Mail**.

c) Identify the elements of the page.
- The subject is "cafes in boston - Bing".
- There is room to add a message.
- Below the message area is the address for the search results you are sharing.

cafes in boston - Bing

Add a message

 cafes in boston - Bing

http://www.bing.com/search?q=cafes+in+boston&src=IE-
TopResult&FORM=IE11TR&conversationid=BB5D353D0DD14C84BF2C0A11AB69EA65

Sent from Windows Mail

- Your email address is at the top of the page.

d) In the **To** text box, type the email address provided by your instructor.

e) Select the **Send** button to send the email.

Student 01
student01-10-17-13@outlook.com

To

After a few moments, the message is sent and the **Share Charm** closes, taking you back to the search results page.

7. Close the café search tab.

a) Select the **Tabs** button on the command bar to open the **Tabs** menu.

b) Verify that there are two tabs open: one shows the museum page from the museum search, and the other shows the results of the café search.

c) Select the **Close** button to close the café tab.

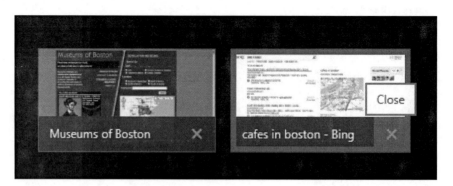

d) Verify that you have returned to the museum page.

e) Select the background of the museum page to close the **Tabs** menu.

8. Keep Internet Explorer open.

TOPIC C

Use Internet Explorer 11 on the Desktop

The Windows Store interface is not the only way to browse with Internet Explorer. You've already worked with the Desktop and some of its apps before, so it's in your best interests to take advantage of the Desktop version of Internet Explorer. Having experience with both versions will make it easier to decide which one suits you best.

Internet Explorer 11 on the Desktop

The Desktop app of Internet Explorer 11 presents the traditional experience users of earlier versions of Windows may be familiar with. Much of the functionality of the Windows Store version of Internet Explorer is shared with its Desktop equivalent; in fact, the Desktop app is somewhat more robust and offers advanced features that the Store version does not. For example, the Desktop app allows users to install third-party programs called *add-ons* or plugins that extend the functionality of the browser, like adding video player software. On the contrary, the Windows Store Internet Explorer app cannot be extended beyond its default browsing tools. The Store app therefore consumes less resources and provides a more secure browsing experience.

As with most Desktop apps, Internet Explorer is contained in a window with various navigation and sizing elements. Visually, the most significant difference between the Desktop and Store apps is that the Desktop version displays more on the screen, whereas the Store version hides controls for a sleeker presentation. All of the navigation elements you used in the Store app are always available from any page at any time.

Even though Internet Explorer on the Desktop is designed to be used separately, it shares settings with the Windows Store variant, and vice versa. For example, if you set your home page in the Desktop app, then the next time you open the Windows Store app, it will start on that page. When you add favorites in the Windows Store app, those same favorites will be listed in the Desktop app.

Figure 4–10: The Internet Explorer 11 Desktop app.

Elements of the Internet Explorer Desktop Window

The following table describes the various elements of an Internet Explorer window on the Desktop.

Browser Element	Description
Page content	This is the body of the window that displays the web page's content, and generally includes text, images, videos, and links to other pages.
Navigation buttons	These buttons allow you navigate backward and forward between web pages, if applicable.
Address bar	As with in the Windows Store app, entering a word or phrase in this field will return search results from Bing. If you enter a specific URL into this same field, you will be taken to that website.
Tabs	You can navigate multiple pages at once in the same browser window. The page you are currently on is the active tab, whereas any other tabs are inactive and can be switched to at any time.
Home	Selecting this icon will take you to whatever your current home page is.
View favorites, feeds, and history	Selecting this icon opens a menu with three tabs. The **Favorites** tab lists any sites you have marked, the **Feeds** tab keeps a frequently updating list of information from the sites you choose to follow, and the **History** tab allows you to find sites you have visited in the past.
Tools	Selecting this icon opens a drop-down menu with options for enhancing and managing your browsing experience. Selecting **Internet options** takes you to a dialog box where much of Internet Explorer's settings can be changed.

Toolbars

Toolbars in the Desktop Internet Explorer app add menus and controls to the window. Many of the options in these menus and controls can be accessed from elsewhere, but placing toolbars in plain sight could make common browsing tasks quicker and easier to complete. There are four toolbars, each with its own set of functions: **Menu**, **Favorites**, **Command**, and **Status**. When you add any of these toolbars to the window, a space is create for the toolbar to reside in. The first three toolbars, which occupy the top of the window, will change orientation based on the presence of the other two toolbars. For example, the **Command** toolbar will be docked in the upper-left of the window until the **Favorites** bar is added, in which case the **Command** bar will slide over to the right. Toolbars can be added or removed at any time.

Figure 4–11: The Menu, Favorites, Command, and Status toolbars.

The following table lists the toolbars available in the Internet Explorer Desktop app, along with their functions.

Toolbar	Functions
Menu	Adds tabs to the window that, when selected, display a drop-down menu of options and commands based on the category of that tab. Almost every function of Internet Explorer is available from this toolbar.
Favorites	Allows you to view a list of your favorites that runs horizontally across the toolbar. Also provides a button for adding new favorites.
Command	Gives an assortment of controls with drop-down menus for printing, managing web pages, changing safety options, and working with miscellaneous browsing tools.
Status	Adds a bar to the bottom of the window that displays the URL of any link, including text, images, and video, that your pointer is hovering over. Also adds a function for zooming in and out of the page.

Internet Options

The **Internet Options** dialog box is the hub from which you can change a wide variety of settings in Internet Explorer. Like many settings-related dialog boxes, **Internet Options** has multiple tabs for different categories of options. Some of the more common settings you can change from this dialog box are:

- Setting a new home page.
- Altering tab appearance and functionality.
- Deleting browsing history and cleaning up saved data.
- Changing page appearance through font size, color, and language.
- Managing how web content is restricted based on the level of trust with a site, privacy concerns, and appropriateness.

There also many more options for advanced users to finely tune their browsing experience.

 Access the Checklist tile on your LogicalCHOICE course screen for reference information and job aids on How to Use Internet Explorer 11 on the Desktop.

ACTIVITY 4–3
Using the Internet Explorer Desktop App

Before You Begin

The Internet Explorer Store app is open and you are browsing the Museums of Boston page.

Scenario

You've found an excellent resource on museums in Boston, and now you'd like to find one that interests you for your trip. However, you think that you'll spend more time working with Desktop apps while simultaneously surfing the web, so you decide to use the Desktop version of Internet Explorer. Before you start following links on this web page, however, you remember hearing stories about people who follow the wrong links on unfamiliar sites and wind up getting a computer virus. So, you'll use the status bar to confirm that the link to the list of museums looks legitimate. After that's done, you'll select a museum from the list and open its own website in a new tab—that way, in case you change your mind, you won't have lost your place in the museum list. After finally deciding on a museum to visit, you want to set a new home page that you think will be a better web portal than MSN for your future browsing sessions.

1. Open the web page in the Desktop version of Internet Explorer 11.
   a) From the command bar, select the **Page tools** icon.

   b) From the pop-up menu, select **View in the desktop**.
      You are taken to the Desktop, and Internet Explorer opens in a Desktop application window.

2. Add the status toolbar and confirm the legitimacy of the link.
   a) Right-click in the space above the **Address** bar to open the Internet Explorer window context menu.

b) Select **Status bar**.

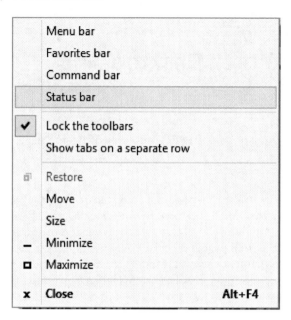

The contextual menu closes and the status bar appears at the bottom of the window, below the scroll bar.

c) Hover your pointer over the **MEMBER MUSEUMS** link on the page.

d) Verify that a URL appears in the status bar. The address appears to be part of the same Museums of Boston website (**www.museumsofboston.org**), and not an unknown or suspicious site.

http://www.museumsofboston.org/search.php?title=Member+Museums+By+Name

e) Select the link to navigate to a page that lists Boston museums by name.

3. Open a link to a museum website in a new tab.

a) Scroll down until you come across a listing titled **HARVARD ART MUSEUMS, Cambridge**.

b) Right-click the **MUSEUM WEBSITE** link next to the listing to open up the link's context menu.

c) From the context menu, select **Open link in new tab**.

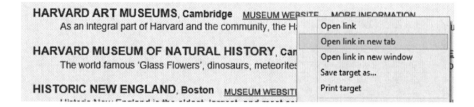

A new, inactive tab opens near the top of the Internet Explorer window.

d) Select the newly added **Harvard Art Museums** tab to open that website.

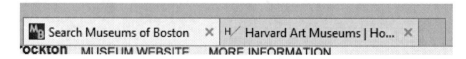

4. Close the newly opened tab and navigate to the museum's information.

a) On the **Harvard Art Museums** tab, select the X to the right to close the tab.

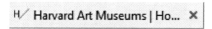

You are returned to the Museums of Boston website, which is now the sole, active tab.

b) Select the **MORE INFORMATION** link for any of the museums listed to go to its information page.

5. Navigate to Google.com.

a) Select the URL in the **Address** bar to highlight it.

 **Note:** Depending on what museum information page you chose in the previous step, your current URL may be different than the one in this image.

b) Type *www.google.com* and press **Enter**.

c) Verify that you are taken to the Google home page.

6. Make Google your home page.

a) From the upper-right corner of the Internet Explorer window, under the **Close** button, select the **Tools** gear icon.

b) From the drop-down menu, select **Internet options**.

Print	▶
File	▶
Zoom (100%)	▶
Safety	▶
Add site to Apps	
View downloads	Ctrl+J
Manage add-ons	
F12 Developer Tools	
Go to pinned sites	
Compatibility View settings	
Internet options	
About Internet Explorer	

The **Internet Options** dialog box opens.

c) From the **General** tab, in the **Home page** section, select the **Use current** button.

d) Verify that the URL in the text box changes to **https://www.google.com/**.

e) Select **OK** to save your changes and close the **Internet Options** dialog box.

7. Verify your new home page.

a) Close the Internet Explorer window.

b) From the taskbar, select the Internet Explorer icon.

c) Verify that Internet Explorer opens to the Google home page.

8. Close Internet Explorer and return to the **Start** screen.

Summary

In this lesson, you opened Internet Explorer 11 as both a Windows Store and Desktop app, and learned how to search the web and share your results. You also learned how to use multiple tabs, navigate between pages, and set preferences and favorites. With these skills, you'll be able to customize your searches to utilize the many resources on the Internet in your workplace and in your personal life.

How might the Share Charm help you in your job?

What version of Internet Explorer would you prefer to use: Store or Desktop? Why?

 Note: Check your LogicalCHOICE Course screen for opportunities to interact with your classmates, peers, and the larger LogicalCHOICE online community about the topics covered in this course or other topics you are interested in. From the Course screen you can also access available resources for a more continuous learning experience.

5 | Customizing the Windows 8.1 Environment

Lesson Time: 1 hour

Lesson Objectives

In this lesson, you will customize the Windows 8.1 environment. You will:

*   Customize the look of the **Start** screen.

*   Customize the look of the Desktop and Desktop applications.

Lesson Introduction

As it is in your office at work, it's nice to be able to customize your PC so that it fits the way you work and reflects your personality. With Microsoft® Windows® 8.1, you can change the colors on your screen, make the pointer easier to work with, make the layout of the **Start** screen more efficient, and control the devices connected to your PC.

TOPIC A

Customize the Start Screen

As you work with Windows 8.1 and add more apps, you'll probably want to organize the tiles to make finding apps easier. You may even want to personalize your PC by changing the look of the **Lock** screen, the **Start** screen, and your Account ID photo. In addition, you'll probably be adding peripherals to your PC or want to clear your search history.

Tile Groups

Tiles on the **Start** screen are laid out in groups, and in the initial setup of Windows 8.1, there are two groups of tiles. As you add apps and pin them to **Start**, this layout may get a bit disorganized. To make tiles easier to find, you can group similar or often-used tiles together in one group, and give the group a name. You can rearrange groups on the **Start** screen, and add or remove tiles from groups as needed. Selecting the **Semantic Zoom** button will zoom out the **Start** screen so you can see all tiles pinned to it. This is handy when you have more tiles than will fit on one screen. This also allows you to move groups of tiles around.

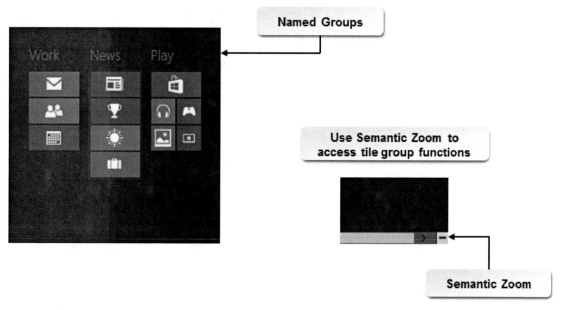

Figure 5-1: Tile groups.

 Access the Checklist tile on your **LogicalCHOICE** course screen for reference information and job aids on **How to Create and Name Tile Groups.**

ACTIVITY 5-1
Creating Groups on the Start Screen

Scenario
In your work, you will probably add apps to the **Start** screen, and you may find that you use some apps more than others. Organizing and labeling groups of tiles will make finding and opening apps much easier in your everyday endeavors. You will organize the apps into related groups.

1. Create a new group.
   a) Select the **News** tile.
   b) Begin dragging the tile to the right until a vertical bar appears. This will create a new group containing the **News** tile.
   c) Add the **Weather, Finance,** and **Sports** tiles to the new group.
   d) Make the **Finance** tile larger and the **Sports** tile wider.
   e) Drag any of the remaining tiles that you want to use frequently (other than the four you just moved) to the left into the group with **Desktop** and **Mail**.
   f) You should now have two groups of tiles.

 Note: It's okay if your **Start** screen doesn't look exactly like this image. The important thing is to have two groups with the correct tiles in each group.

 Note: Your computer might contain additional groups of tiles such as tiles for Microsoft Office applications, games, and pre-installed software added by the computer manufacturer.

2. Name the group.
   a) Right-click any blank area on the **Start** screen.
   b) Select **Name groups.**
   c) Select the **Name group** text box above the group on the right with the **News** and **Weather** apps.

    d) Type *News* and press **Enter**.

    e) Select anywhere on the background to return **Start** to normal.

    f) Verify that the group on the right is now named **News**.

3. Move the group.

    a) Use the **Semantic Zoom** button to zoom out the **Start** screen and view all groups.

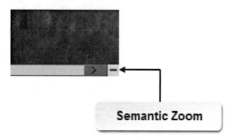

    b) Drag the **News** group to the left side of the screen. The other group will move to accommodate the new location.

    c) Select anywhere on the screen to return **Start** to full size.

    d) Confirm that the groups are rearranged and the **News** group is now the group on the left.

The Settings Charm

Like the **Share Charm**, the **Settings Charm** is context sensitive and offers different options depending on where you are when you open it. On the **Start** screen, the **Settings Charm** lets you personalize the colors and background pattern of the **Start** screen. You're also given the ability to clear any personal information from your **Start** tiles. This doesn't turn live tiles off, but resets the tiles to their default state. No matter where you are, the **Settings Charm** enables you to perform several actions:

- Access **Shut down** options.
- View Wi-Fi signal strength and connect to a network.
- Adjust speaker volume.
- Change the frequency of notifications.
- Access the onscreen keyboard.
- Adjust the brightness of your monitor.
- Access **Help**, which opens a browser to Microsoft's tutorial website.
- Change your computer's settings.

Change PC Settings

Accessed through the **Settings Charm, Change PC settings** is a collection of menus that gives you control over many aspects of how your PC looks and works. From the appearance of the **Start** screen to adding new users or devices, the **PC settings** menu gives you access to menus for changing time zone and language, managing network connections, deleting search history, changing passwords and privacy settings, and much more.

Like Desktop File Explorer, the **PC settings** menu has a **Navigation** pane displaying menus and submenus on the left side of the screen, and a **Contents** pane on the right displaying the actions available for the selected menu or submenu. **PC settings** also has a dedicated search bar, allowing you to search for a specific function without needing to navigate through the menus.

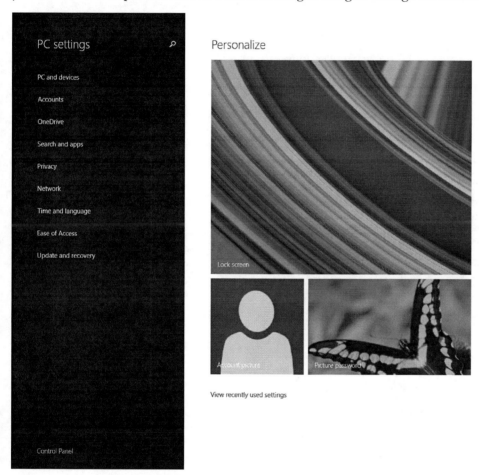

Figure 5-2: The PC settings menu.

PC Settings Menus

The following table is a list of the various menus available in **PC settings**.

Menu	Uses
PC and devices	Allows you to change the pictures used for the **Lock** screen background, and decide which apps can post status notifications on the **Lock** screen. Also enables you to adjust display preferences; add or remove devices such as printers, keyboards, and external storage drives; turn on or off autocorrect and misspelling highlighting; adjust mouse and touchpad settings; configure how screen corners and edges are used for app switching and navigation; choose when your computer turns off its screen and goes into sleep mode; and how AutoPlay handles opening external devices. You can view how much space is disk space is available and how much is taken up by media and files, and by the **Recycle Bin**. Your computer's basic information, like its processor type, random access memory (RAM), and PC name, are also available.
Accounts	Allows you to select or create an account picture and access account settings online. You can change your password and set up PIN and picture passwords, and set whether passwords must be used when resuming from sleep mode. Also enables you to add user accounts to the PC.
OneDrive	Shows you how much space is on your OneDrive account, and allows you to personalize what files and app settings are synchronized with your account.
Search and apps	Allows you to modify how and if Bing personalizes your search experience with suggestions, as well as adjusting content filters and clearing search history. Enables you to turn app notifications on or off, and indicate which apps may show notifications. You can also customize which apps can take advantage of sharing features, uninstall Windows Store apps from your computer, and choose which programs default to opening certain types of files.
Privacy	Lets you control whether apps can use your location, name, and account picture, and whether Microsoft can use the URLs from websites you use to help select apps for the Windows Store. You can also allow or disallow apps from using devices connected to your computer, such as a webcam or microphone.
Network	Lets you adjust your Internet connections, set up a connection proxy, and connect two or more PCs on a home network in order to share printers, media, and document libraries. Also allows you to join a workplace to access network resources or allow your IT admin to set up apps and services.
Time and language	Enables you to set your time zone, change the format of dates and times, and have the PC automatically adjust for daylight saving time. Also allows you to set your country or region, and add languages.
Ease of Access	Allows you to set **Ease of Access** features such as **Narrator**, **Magnifier**, **High contrast** monitor, on-screen keyboard, and cursor thickness. Also lets you adjust how long notifications remain on your screen.
Update and recovery	Although Windows is set up to automatically search for and install updates, this allows you to manually check for updates. You're also given the option to back up your files or restore your computer to a previous state in case it isn't running properly.

 Note: You can also remove flash drives and other external storage devices via the **Notification** area on the Desktop.

Access to the **Control Panel** is also available from the **PC settings** navigation pane. Selecting this option opens the **Control Panel** on the Desktop. You can use **Control Panel** to change the same settings as you can through **PC settings** and also other settings that aren't included in **PC settings.**

 Access the Checklist tile on your LogicalCHOICE course screen for reference information and job aids on How to Change Common Elements of the Windows 8.1 Environment.

ACTIVITY 5-2
Changing PC Settings

Before You Begin

Have your password handy, as you will be locking your account during this activity and you will need it to sign back in to your account.

Scenario

You customized the **Start** screen by grouping tiles and arranging and naming the groups. Now, you'll continue to customize Windows 8.1 by changing the backgrounds for the **Lock** and **Start** screens, adding an app notification to the **Lock** screen, selecting your time zone, and clearing all of your personal info from live tiles. These changes can make using Windows 8.1 more enjoyable and useful.

---

1. Access the **PC settings** menu.
   a) Select the **Settings Charm**.
   b) On the bottom of the **Settings** menu, select **Change PC settings** to open the **PC settings** menu.

   c) In the **Navigation** pane, select **PC and devices**.
   d) In the **Navigation** pane, verify that **Lock screen** is selected and that the large picture in the preview area shows how the **Lock** screen currently looks.

2. Change the **Lock** screen background picture.
   a) Below the preview picture, view the optional pictures supplied for that screen.
   b) Select each of the smaller pictures to see how the **Lock** screen will look with that picture.
   c) Select the picture you wish to use for the **Lock** screen background.

3. Add an app notification to appear on the **Lock** screen.

a) Under **Lock screen apps**, verify that several apps are listed under **Choose apps to run in the background and show quick status and notifications, even when your screen is locked.**

Lock screen apps

Choose apps to run in the background and show quick status and notifications, even when your screen is locked

b) Select the icon under **Choose an app to display detailed status**.

Choose an app to display detailed status

c) From the pop-up menu, select **Weather**.

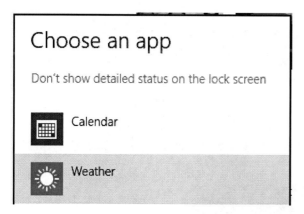

Choose an app

Don't show detailed status on the lock screen

Calendar

Weather

4. Lock your account to view the changes to the **Lock** screen.

   a) Return to the **Start** screen.
   b) Select your **Account ID** to open the menu.
   c) Select **Lock**.
   d) Verify that the new picture you chose is now the **Lock** screen background.
   e) Confirm that detailed weather information is displayed next to the time.

5. Change the time zone.

   a) Select anywhere on the **Lock** screen and sign in to your account.
   b) From the **Settings Charm**, select **Change PC settings**.
   c) In the **Navigation** pane, select the **Back** button, and then select **Time and language**.

d) Under **Date and time**, select the **Time zone** drop-down list to display the time zones available.

Time zone

(UTC-05:00) Eastern Time (US & Canada)   ⌄

e) From the options listed, select your time zone. If necessary, use the scroll bar on the right side of the menu to view your time zone.

6. If necessary, select the switch below the time zone to toggle daylight saving time to **On**.

Adjust for daylight saving time automatically

On

7. Select the **Back** button in the **Navigation** pane to return to the main **PC settings** screen.

8. Return to the **Start** screen.

9. Display the **Charms** menu to view the time. If you had to change time zones, the new time should now be displayed.

10. Change the **Start** screen background.
    a) Select the **Settings Charm**.
    b) Under **Settings**, select **Personalize**.
    c) In the **Personalize** pane, verify that there is an assortment of stylized graphics and colors.
    d) Select the graphics to see how the **Start** screen would look with a different graphic.

    e) Below the graphics options, observe the **Background color** options.

f) Select some of the color options to see the **Start** screen using different background colors.

Background color

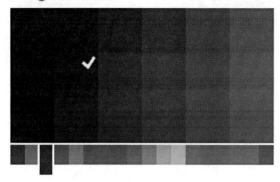

g) From the **Accent color** options, select some of the colors to see the accent color change.

Accent color

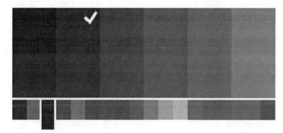

h) Select the graphic and color option you wish to use for the **Start** screen background.

 Note: Your changes are automatically saved.

11. Clear personal information from live tiles.
    a) From the **Personalize** pane, select the **Back** button.
    b) Under **Settings**, select **Tiles**.

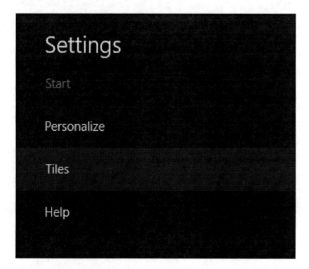

c) Select **Clear** to clear personal information from the tiles.

Show administrative tools

No

Clear personal info from my tiles

d) Verify that the tiles are reset.
e) Close the menu to return to **Start**.

TOPIC B

Customize the Desktop

Besides changing the **Lock** and **Start** screens, you can also change the look of several different Desktop elements. Because many of the apps you'll be using are exclusive to the Desktop, you'll want to personalize this space so you can be more comfortable using it. In this topic, you'll adjust the Desktop so that it reflects your own individual tastes.

Desktop Background

When you open the Desktop, the background shows the default picture that comes with Windows 8.1. You can change the background picture by using other pictures bundled with Windows 8.1, or by using your own pictures. You can select one picture to be displayed, or have several displayed as a slide show, with the interval between pictures ranging from 10 seconds to one day. Windows 8.1 also offers high-contrast backgrounds, for easier-to-see, less-cluttered viewing. Pictures can be positioned on your screen in the numerous ways:

*   **Fill**—The picture will fill the entire screen. Some stretching or picture loss may occur.
*   **Fit**—The picture will fit the screen horizontally, but may have black areas above and below.
*   **Stretch**—The picture will be stretched to cover the screen top to bottom or side to side.
*   **Tile**—Many small copies of the picture will cover the screen in a tiled fashion.
*   **Center**—The picture will be centered on your screen with black on all sides.

You can use the same background picture on the Desktop and the **Start** screen. This can be configured through the **Personalization** option selected from the **Start** screen or through the **Taskbar and Navigation properties** dialog box from the Desktop.

The background you select is tied to your login account. If you are using a Microsoft ID login account rather than a local account, if you log in with your Microsoft ID account on another computer, the background you last selected when you were logged in on any computer is the background that will be displayed.

Border and Taskbar Color

You can also change the color and intensity of the borders of windows and the taskbar. Windows 8.1 offers 16 different colors to choose from. Changing the window color will affect the title bar, borders, and taskbar. You can save picture and border color combinations as **Themes**, making switching between customizations easier.

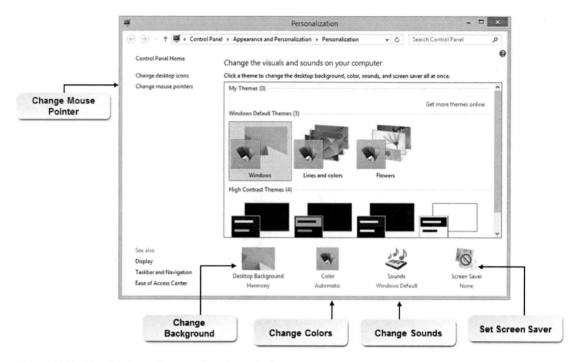

Figure 5-3: The Desktop Personalization window.

Screen Savers

With early models of PCs and monitors, if you left a static image on your monitor for too long, the image would burn into your screen. To combat this, *screen savers* were developed. Screen savers provide either a blank screen, or a constant changing of images or words on your monitor. This constant refreshing of your monitor prevents image burn. When your computer has not been used for a specified amount of time, the screen saver will start up and will continue to be displayed until you either move your mouse or press a key on your keyboard. Image burn isn't as much a problem with modern PCs, as they have sleep mode, which blanks out the monitor after a specified amount of time. However, some people still like to use screen savers.

 Note: Screen savers don't really serve a purpose anymore; they're just fun.

 Access the Checklist tile on your LogicalCHOICE course screen for reference information and job aids on How to Customize the Desktop.

Pointers

When you first use Windows, the default pointer shape is a white arrow. As your pointer moves over aspects of the screen, it changes shape according to the field or action that you can perform. To make viewing and tracking the pointer easier, you can change the size, shape, and color of your pointer. You can also set it so that your pointer has a shadow or has pointer trails. With pointer trails, whenever you move your pointer you will see several pointers "following" it. This makes it easier for your eyes to track the pointer movement. You can also set the pointer to move faster or slower in relation to your mouse movement. Use the **Mouse Properties** dialog box to change other pointer properties, such as button configuration and click speed.

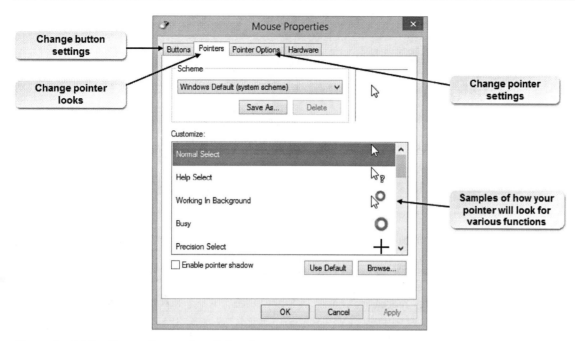

Figure 5-4: The Mouse Properties dialog box.

 Access the Checklist tile on your LogicalCHOICE course screen for reference information and job aids on How to Customize Your Pointer.

ACTIVITY 5-3
Personalizing the Desktop

Before You Begin
You are on the **Start** screen.

Scenario
Studies have shown that when you personalize your workspace, you enjoy work more and you work more efficiently. To help keep yourself motivated throughout the day, you decide to make your Desktop as visually pleasing to you as possible. You're not sure you really like the default yellow coloring to the Windows 8.1 Desktop, so you decide to change your background and the color of the taskbar and windows. Although you know having a screen saver doesn't offer much practical benefit, you like to leave a personalized message displayed on your screen when you're out to lunch. Finally, you use the mouse so often that you want to choose the best on-screen speed to maximize your ability to navigate with it. You even consider adding trails to your pointer to make it easier to see.

---

1. Change the Desktop background.
   a) Select the **Desktop** tile to open the Desktop app.
   b) On the Desktop, select the **Settings Charm**.
   c) Select **Personalization**.

   d) Select **Desktop Background** to view the Windows 8.1 default pictures.

   Desktop Background
   Harmony

   e) In the section with picture samples, scroll up to view more available background pictures.
   f) Select the picture that you prefer.
   g) Verify that the Desktop changes to show how the picture will look.

Note: You may want to minimize the window to view the new picture on the Desktop. Restore the window when you are done viewing the Desktop. Also, notice that the sample pictures have their own themes, which changes the color of the taskbar and your window borders when you use these pictures.

h) When you have chosen a picture to use, select **Save changes** to make the new picture your Desktop background.

2. Change the window and taskbar color.

a) In the Personalization window, select **Color** to access the Color and Appearance window.

Color

Automatic

b) Select a color from the array.
c) Verify that the window borders and taskbar change to that color.
d) Drag the **Color intensity** slider to change the intensity of the color.

Color intensity:

e) Confirm that the color of the borders and taskbar changes intensity.
f) When you have adjusted the color and intensity to your liking, select **Save changes** to keep the changes and return to the Personalization window.

3. Select a screen saver.

a) In the Personalization window, select **Screen Saver** to access the **Screen Saver Settings** dialog box.
b) In the **Screen saver** section, verify that the **Screen saver** setting is set to **(None)**.

Screen saver

| (None) | ⌄ | Settings... | Preview |

c) For **Screen saver**, select the down arrow to view available screen savers.
d) Select the **3D Text** screen saver.
e) In the **Screen saver** section, select **Settings**.

Screen saver

| 3D Text | ⌄ | Settings... | Preview |

f) In the **3D Text Settings** dialog box, in the **Text** section, confirm that the **Custom Text** radio button is selected.

g) In the **Custom Text** radio button text box, select **Windows 8.1** to highlight it.

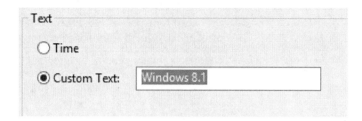

h) Type the following: *Out to lunch until 1*
i) Select **OK**.
j) In the **Screen saver** section, select **Preview**.
k) Confirm that the out-to-lunch message is now the screen saver.
l) Move the pointer to exit the preview and return to the **Screen Saver Settings** dialog box.
m) In the **Screen saver** section, in the **Wait** spin box, select the up arrow to change how long your PC needs to be idle before the screen saver is displayed to 10 minutes.

n) Select **OK** to save changes and close the **Screen Saver Settings** dialog box.

4. Change the pointer shape.
   a) In the Personalization window **Navigation** pane, select **Change mouse pointers** to open the **Mouse Properties** dialog box.
   b) In the display box near the top-right of the window, verify that the default pointer is shown.
   c) In the **Customize** box, scroll to view the current pointer shapes.
   d) In the **Scheme** section, verify that **Windows Default (system scheme)** is listed.

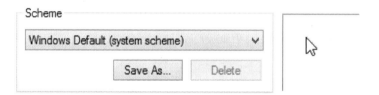

e) Select the **Scheme** down arrow to view a list of available pointer schemes.
   f) From the list, select a pointer scheme option.
   g) In the display box, verify that the pointer changes shape.
   h) In the **Customize** box, confirm that the shapes have changed as well.
   i) Select **Apply** to accept the new scheme.
   j) Confirm that your pointer changes to the new shape.

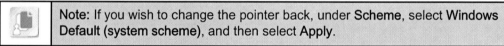

Note: If you wish to change the pointer back, under **Scheme**, select **Windows Default (system scheme)**, and then select **Apply**.

k) If necessary, select the **Mouse Properties** dialog box to make it your active window.

5. Change pointer motion options.

a) At the top of the **Mouse Properties** dialog box, select **Pointer Options**.

b) In the **Motion** section, drag the **Motion** slider to **Slow**.
c) Move your pointer around to verify that your pointer now moves more slowly in relation to your mouse movements.
d) Drag the **Motion** slider to **Fast**, and move your pointer to verify that it now moves faster.
e) Drag the slider to a point you prefer.

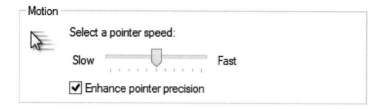

f) In the **Visibility** section, check the **Display pointer trails** check box.

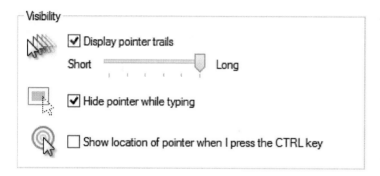

g) Move your pointer. It is followed by a trail of pointers.
h) Uncheck **Display pointer trails**. (You may skip this step if you like having the trails on.)
i) Select **OK** to save changes and close the **Mouse Properties** dialog box.

6. Close the Personalization window and return to the **Start** screen.

Summary

In this lesson, you customized your PC so that it fits the way you work and reflects your personality. You changed the visual appeal of the Desktop and made the layout of the **Start** screen more efficient. With these changes in place, you'll be able to settle into a new work environment as painlessly as possible.

Why might you customize the look of your computer and pointer?

How might creating groups of tiles help you in your day-to-day work?

 Note: Check your LogicalCHOICE Course screen for opportunities to interact with your classmates, peers, and the larger LogicalCHOICE online community about the topics covered in this course or other topics you are interested in. From the Course screen you can also access available resources for a more continuous learning experience.

6 | Using Windows 8.1 Security Features

Lesson Time: 50 minutes

Lesson Objectives

In this lesson, you will use Windows 8.1 security features. You will:

- Set privacy levels and set and change your passwords.

- Use Windows Defender.

- Open OneDrive and synchronize a file.

Lesson Introduction

The security of your PC, data, and privacy are very important in today's world. With Microsoft® Windows® 8.1, you can manage your privacy and protect your PC from unauthorized access, store and back up your files, and even safely share your files with others.

TOPIC A

Set Privacy Levels and Passwords

As you saw earlier in the course, passwords can help keep your account protected. In addition to using passwords to protect the data on your PC, you can limit how other personal information is accessed.

Passwords

Although you use a password to protect your PC, hackers are relentless when it comes to trying to steal your information. Periodically changing your password can go a long way toward thwarting them. To give you more options for signing in, Windows 8.1 allows you to create a picture password or a PIN password for faster sign-in. The default sign-in for a Microsoft Account is the eight-character password. A picture password will replace that. If you create a PIN password, it will take precedence over both the regular password and the picture password. However, at sign-in, you can select which option you wish to use by selecting **Sign-in options** from the **Accounts** settings menu. To ensure that no one can change your password and lock you out, you must enter your current password whenever you make a password change.

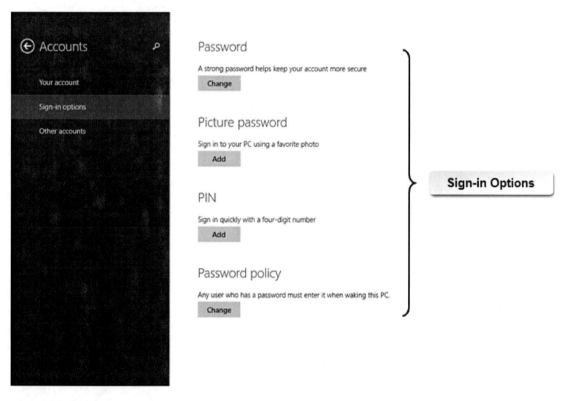

Figure 6–1: The sign-in options in PC settings.

PIN Passwords

PIN passwords are four numbers long, making signing in quicker and easier. When you use the PIN password, you type in the numbers, but do not need to press **Enter**. Once you type the last number, you are automatically signed in.

Picture Passwords

With the picture password, you specify the picture and "draw" motions on the picture as the password. These motions can be any combination of taps, straight lines, and circles; and the size, position, direction, and order in which you make the motions combine to become your password. Because some hackers use programs that record your keystrokes, giving them access to your eight-character password or four-digit PIN, the motions used in picture passwords offer another level of security.

Figure 6–2: Three gestures on a picture password.

 Access the Checklist tile on your LogicalCHOICE course screen for reference information and job aids on How to Use Passwords.

ACTIVITY 6–1
Changing Your Password

Data Files
This PC\Pictures\picture_password.png

Before You Begin
You are at the **Start** screen.

Scenario
To protect against data loss and identity theft, your company is now requiring employees to change their account passwords regularly. You'll create a PIN password, change your current password, and create a picture password. You will then sign in using each of the new passwords. Knowing how to create and use all three types of passwords will enable you to vary your sign-in procedure and keep your data, identity, and PC better protected.

---

1. Change your password.
   a) Select the **Settings Charm**.
   b) Select **Change PC settings**.
   c) In the **Navigation** pane of **PC settings**, select **Accounts**.

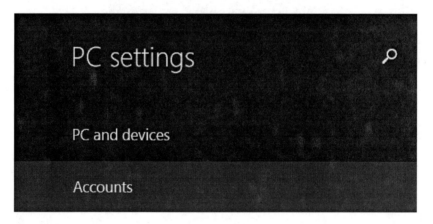

   d) From the **Navigation** pane, select **Sign-in options**.
   e) Confirm that the **Contents** pane contains options for changing and adding passwords.
   f) In the **Contents** pane, under **Password**, select **Change** to open the **Sign in to your Microsoft account** screen.
   g) In the text box, type *win8class* and select **Finish** to verify your account.
   h) From the **Change your Microsoft account password** screen, in the **Old password** text box, type *win8class*
   i) In the **New password** text box, type *Win8cl@ss*
   j) In the **Reenter password** text box, type *Win8cl@ss*
   k) Select **Next**.
   l) When prompted, select **Finish**.

2. Create a PIN password.

---

a) In the **Contents** pane, under **PIN**, select **Add**.

PIN

Sign in quickly with a four-digit number

Add

b) Verify that the **Create a PIN** screen is displayed.
c) On the **Create a PIN** screen, in the **Password** text box, type *Win8cl@ss* and select **OK**.

d) In the **Enter PIN** text box, type *1234*
e) In the **Confirm PIN** text box, type *1234*

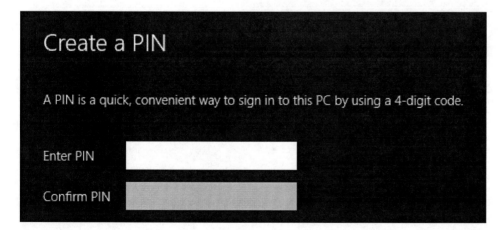

f) Select **Finish**.

 Note: When you do this on your PC, it's a good idea to use random numbers to make it harder for a hacker to figure out. For our purposes here, 1234 is fine.

g) In the **Contents** pane, verify that there are now options to **Change** and to **Remove** the PIN.
h) Return to **Start**.

      i)   Use your **Account ID** menu to select **Lock**.

      j)   Select anywhere to display the **Sign In** screen.

      k)   Confirm that the **Password** text box now says **PIN**.

      l)   In the **Password** text box, type *1234* to sign in.

      m) Verify that you are signed in and are viewing the **Start** screen.

3. Create a picture password.

      a) Use the **Switcher** to navigate to **PC settings**.

      b) In the **Navigation** pane of **Accounts**, confirm that **Sign-in options** is selected.

      c) In the **Contents** pane, under **Picture password**, select **Add**.

      d) On the **Create a picture password** screen, in the **Password** text box, type *Win8cl@ss*

      e) Select **OK**.

      f)   Confirm that you are viewing the **Welcome to picture password** screen.

      g) Verify that the motions shown on the example picture are a line, a circle, and a tap.

      h) Select **Choose picture** to open your **Pictures** folder.

      i)   In the **Pictures** folder, select the **Butterfly** picture.

      j)   Select **Open**.

      k) If necessary, drag the picture to position it so you can see both wings.

l)   Select **Use this picture**.

m) Starting at the top of the right wing, select and drag your pointer toward the body, along the vertical line of yellow dots.

n)   Starting at the top of the left wing, select and drag your pointer toward the body, along the upper line of yellow dots.

o)   Starting at the head of the butterfly, select and drag your pointer along the body toward the orange spots.

p)   When prompted, repeat the three gestures in order to confirm them. If you make a mistake, select **Start over**.

q)   Select **Finish** to go back to **PC settings**.

r)   From the **Navigation** pane, select the **Back** button to return to the main **PC settings** menu.

4. Sign in using your new picture password.

a)   Return to **Start**.

b)   Using your **Account ID** menu, select **Lock**.

c)   Select anywhere to display the **Sign In** screen.

d)   Confirm that your picture appears, along with the option to switch to your password.

e)   Select **Switch to password**.

f)   Below the **Password** text box, select **Sign-in options**.

g)   Confirm that the options show three icons: a picture of mountains, a PIN pad, and a key.

h)   Select the PIN pad.

i)   Verify that the password text box now says **PIN**.

j)   Select the mountains icon. You are taken to the picture password screen.

k)   Draw your three gestures on the butterfly to sign in. If you make a mistake, you can select **Start over** and try again.

l)   Verify that you are returned to the **Start** screen.

Privacy

Although allowing websites to track your location can give you a more tailored online experience, there will be times when you will want to maintain your privacy. Along with limiting access to location, you can decide whether or not apps can use your name and account picture, and whether to let Microsoft keep track of what websites you visit for use in determining what apps to provide in the Windows Store. Although you may trust some websites to keep your personal information protected, other sites may not be as trustworthy, and denying access to your information is one step toward protecting yourself.

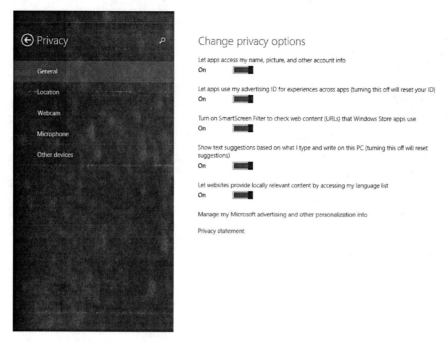

Figure 6-3: The Privacy settings menu.

The following table describes general privacy settings that you may turn on or off in Windows 8.1.

Privacy Setting	Description
Let apps access my name, picture, and other account info	This toggles whether or not Windows Store apps can use the information of the account you're logged in with. Apps like Mail and People typically use your name and picture to personalize the way you communicate.
Let apps use my advertising ID for experiences across apps	When you use a Microsoft Account with Windows 8.1, you are also assigned an advertising ID that is tied to your account. When this setting is on, the advertisements that you see in Windows Store apps will be tailored to your interests based on your personal information. When toggled off, you will still see ads, but they won't be specifically tailored for you.
Turn on SmartScreen Filter to check web content (URLs) that Windows Store apps use	SmartScreen Filter is a function in Internet Explorer that attempts to block websites it determines are suspicious and may harm your computer. With this setting on, SmartScreen Filter will offer this protection in other apps that try to access the Web. It is not recommended you turn this setting off.
Show suggestions based on what I type and write on this PC	When this is toggled on, Windows 8.1 will offer suggested words or phrases in places like search boxes. This is based on the text you have entered in the past.
Let websites provide locally relevant content by accessing my language list	Some Windows Store apps provide content that changes based on what languages you have tied to your account. Toggling this setting on allows those apps to display that content, if your account meets the language criteria.
Manage my Microsoft advertising and other personalization info	Selecting this link will open a web page in Internet Explorer 11 where you can further manage if and how your advertising ID is used to tailor ads to your personality and interests.

Privacy Setting	Description
Privacy statement	Selecting this link will open up Microsoft's privacy statement in Internet Explorer 11.

 Access the Checklist tile on your LogicalCHOICE course screen for reference information and job aids on How to Change Privacy Settings.

ACTIVITY 6-2
Changing Privacy Settings

Scenario

Due to ongoing security concerns, your company is limiting how employees share information. Controlling how your information is used is another step in protecting your identity. You will change your privacy settings to disable name, account picture, and web use information sharing.

---

1. Access privacy settings.
   a) Select the **Settings Charm**.
   b) Select **Change PC settings**.
   c) In the **Navigation** pane, select **Privacy**.
   d) In the **Navigation** pane, select **Location**.

2. Disable sharing features.
   a) From the **Contents** pane, if necessary, select the toggle for **Let Windows and apps use my location** to turn it **Off**.

   Let Windows and apps use my location
   Off

   b) In the **Navigation** pane, select **General**.
   c) If necessary, select the toggle for **Let apps access my name, picture, and other account info** to turn it **Off**.

   Let apps access my name, picture, and other account info
   Off

   d) If necessary, select the toggle for **Turn on SmartScreen Filter** to turn it **Off**.

   Turn on SmartScreen Filter to check web content (URLs) that Windows Store apps use
   Off

   e) Verify that there is a **Manage my Microsoft advertising and other personalization info** link.
   f) Verify that there is a **Privacy statement** link.
   g) From the **Navigation** pane, select the **Back** button to return to the main **PC settings** menu.
   h) Return to **Start**.

TOPIC B

Use Windows Defender

Although the Internet is an amazing tool that provides you with access to an astounding amount of content, there are also dangers associated with surfing the web. Without even knowing it, you can infect your computer with malicious software and other dangerous elements. In order to productively benefit from the resources available online, you need to ensure your computer is safe from threats. Windows 8.1 comes loaded with built-in protection against such threats: Windows Defender. Understanding how to use this security tool can help ease your mind as you take advantage of everything the Internet has to offer.

Windows Defender

Whenever you connect to the Internet or open email from unknown senders, your computer is vulnerable to viruses, malicious software (malware), spyware, and unwanted pop-up windows. Many of these unwanted programs can steal the information on your computer, record your keystrokes (a way of recording your passwords), cause damage to your computer, and slow the performance of your PC. *Windows Defender* is a free Microsoft program that protects your computer from unwanted software downloads, and removes and quarantines any that it finds on your hard drive. It is a good idea to run Windows Defender to create a *restore point* while everything is working well on your computer, and routinely update that restore point. This enables you to restore your computer to a working point if it becomes infected with unwanted software.

You can have Windows Defender **Real-time protection** running in the background, so that whenever any unwanted software tries to install itself on your computer, you will be alerted. Many times, viruses are attached to email, and users unwittingly download them when they open these attachments. **Real-time protection** scans attachments and alerts you when it finds anything suspicious. Because hackers are constantly creating new versions of these programs, Windows Defender automatically updates new definitions of potentially dangerous software. You also have the option of performing a manual update to get new definitions as quickly as possible. When Windows 8.1 is installed, Windows Defender is on by default.

 Note: Windows Defender is turned on or off for the PC, so if you have multiple accounts and one user turns it off, it is off for all accounts on that PC.

Figure 6-4: Windows Defender.

Windows Defender Tabs

The following table describes the various tabs available in the Windows Defender app.

Tab	Allows You To
Home	Choose the type of scan to run (**Quick**, **Full**, or **Custom**) and begin running it. You can also view your current protection status and the basic details of past scans, if any.
Update	Update your virus and spyware definitions, view the exact date and time that you last updated them, and view the version numbers of the definitions.
History	View detailed information about any items that have been detected as malware in past scans, items that have been **Quarantined** (stopped from running, but still exist on your computer), and items that you specifically have allowed Windows Defender to ignore.
Settings	Change various settings, including turning **Real-time protection** on or off, excluding certain files or file types from being scanned, and choosing whether or not to send malware information to Microsoft. You may also set options for greater control over scanning and how detected items are handled.

> Access the Checklist tile on your LogicalCHOICE course screen for reference information and job aids on How to Use Windows Defender.

ACTIVITY 6-3
Changing Windows Defender Settings

Scenario

There may be times when you find that your PC has been running a bit slow, or you need to change some of the settings in Windows Defender to customize your protection, to scan removable devices, or create a restore point. You will open Windows Defender, identify the options available, and run a quick scan. Knowing how to work with Windows Defender will help keep your PC and the data it contains protected.

1. Open Windows Defender.
   a) From the **Start** screen, select the **Apps View** down arrow.
   b) On the **Apps View** screen, under the **Windows System** programs, select **Windows Defender** to open the program.

 Note: You may need to scroll to the right to see the **Windows System** apps.

   c) Verify that Windows Defender opens on the Desktop.
   d) In the Windows Defender window, observe the tabs: **Home**, **Update**, **History**, and **Settings**.

2. Determine the status of your protection.
   a) If necessary, select the **Home** tab.
   b) Verify that **Real-time protection** is on.
   c) Verify that your virus and spyware definitions are up to date.

> Real-time protection: **On**
> Virus and spyware definitions: **Up to date**

   d) Identify the scan options. Hold your pointer over the scan options to the right to view the pop-up description.
   e) On the bottom of the **Home** tab, determine whether or not any scans have run.

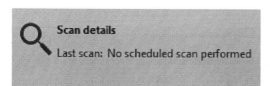

> **Scan details**
> Last scan: No scheduled scan performed

 Note: Depending on how long ago Windows was installed on your PC, Windows Defender may have run a scan automatically. In this case, you'll see the date and time Windows Defender last scanned your computer.

3. Verify your malware definitions are up to date.
    a) Select the **Update** tab.
    b) Next to **Virus and spyware definitions**, verify that there is green text that says **Up to date**.
    c) Confirm that the **Definitions last updated** date is within the last few days.

Virus and spyware definitions: Up to date

Your virus and spyware definitions are automatically updated to help protect your PC.

Definitions created on:	10/10/2013 at 6:04 PM
Definitions last updated:	10/11/2013 at 2:46 PM
Virus definition version:	1.159.1955.0
Spyware definition version:	1.159.1955.0

Update

4. Confirm settings.
    a) Select the **Settings** tab.
    b) If necessary, in the **Navigation** pane, select **Real-time protection**.
    c) Verify that **Turn on real-time protection** is checked.
    d) In the **Navigation** pane, select **Advanced**.
    e) Identify the actions that can be taken on this menu.
    f) In the **Navigation** pane, select **Administrator**.
    g) Verify that **Turn on this app** is checked.

5. (Optional) Run a quick scan.
    a) Select the **Home** tab.
    b) Under **Scan options**, if necessary, select **Quick**.
    c) Select the **Scan now** button to begin the scan.
    d) Verify the number of items scanned.

6. Close the Windows Defender window and return to **Start**.

TOPIC C

Store and Share Files with OneDrive

In your work, you've probably needed to share files with your coworkers, or taken a document home to work on it. With OneDrive, you'll have more flexibility in how you accomplish that. You should also be aware of the risk of data loss, and how to take advantage of OneDrive to back up your important files in case of hardware theft or failure.

OneDrive

You've probably heard people talking about the "cloud" and *cloud computing* and wondered what it was all about. Basically, when you access the cloud, you are making use of hardware and software computing resources that are available over the Internet. The term "cloud" is used as a metaphor to give people an easy-to-understand image of the infrastructure of the Internet. Cloud storage services, such as Microsoft *OneDrive*, typically charge fees based on how much storage space you wish to use, and many give you a certain amount of space for free to get you started. OneDrive comes bundled with Windows 8.1 and is configured with a **Documents** folder. You can add more folders as needed. To use OneDrive, you need to have a Microsoft Account.

 Note: Microsoft Accounts are discussed in the "Other Windows 8.1 Features" appendix.

 Note: OneDrive was previously known as SkyDrive and you might see SkyDrive in some documentation and in some file paths.

You can access your files on OneDrive from your PC, smartphone, or by signing in to your OneDrive account from any computer. When you synchronize a device with OneDrive, it will keep files up to date on both your local machine and in the cloud. The local copies can be accessed with File Explorer in the directory named **OneDrive**. In order to synchronize a file or folder, it must be added to OneDrive and made available offline.

When you open a file on OneDrive from your PC, it will be opened using the appropriate program, or you may choose which program to open it with. While the file is open, any changes that you make and then save will be sent to the cloud, where they can be quickly and easily retrieved. OneDrive also allows you to share files via email by using the **Share Charm**. The OneDrive website, **OneDrive.com**, includes a way to share files by creating groups and inviting others to those groups. More than just the benefits of accessibility and sharing, OneDrive is a good resource for backing up your data. Whether it's due to hardware failing or your computer being stolen, you can lose data instantly and without any warning. Backing up your files to the cloud means that in these events, your hard work will not have been lost to you.

Figure 6-5: The OneDrive main screen.

 Access the Checklist tile on your LogicalCHOICE course screen for reference information and job aids on How to Use OneDrive.

ACTIVITY 6-4
Uploading a File to OneDrive

Data Files

This PC\Desktop\Works in progress\Mental Fitness_revised

Scenario

Now that you've revised the article that's soon to be published in the Bit by Bit Fitness newsletter, you'd like to make absolutely certain that you don't lose it. You decide to create a back up of the article in the cloud, where you can access it at any time with any device. Not only will this save you work in case your computer's hard drive fails, but you can also easily keep editing the file when you're working at home, away from your office computer. Shortly after you open the OneDrive app and synchronize the **Mental Fitness_revised** document, you get an email from your boss stating that the opening of the new children's fitness program is being pushed back a week. You'll need to update the article to reflect this change, and when you do, you'll confirm that the changes synchronized with OneDrive.

1. Upload the **Mental Fitness_revised** document to OneDrive.
   a) Select the **OneDrive** tile to open the app.

   b) If necessary, sign in with your assigned Microsoft Account user name and password.
   c) Select the **Documents** folder.

   d) Right-click to display the command bar.

e) Select **Add files** to open **This PC**.

f) Verify that OneDrive is showing the folders and drives contained in **This PC**.

g) From the list of folders and drives, select **Desktop** to open that location.

h) Select the **Works in progress** folder to open it.

i) Select the **Mental Fitness_revised** file.

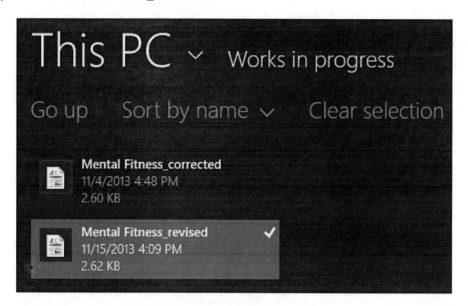

j) Select **Copy to OneDrive** to begin uploading the file.

k) Verify that the **Mental Fitness_revised** file is now in the OneDrive **Documents** folder.

2. Alter your synchronized local copy of the file.
   a) Navigate to the Desktop.
   b) From the taskbar, select the **File Explorer** icon.
   c) From the **Navigation** pane, select **OneDrive**, then open the **Documents** folder.

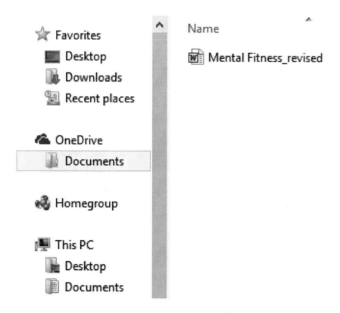

d) Double-click the **Mental Fitness_revised** file to open it in WordPad.
e) In the text, at the very bottom, locate **13th** in the phrase "Our new program will start on Monday, January 13th..."
f) Change **13th** to *20th*

g) Select the save icon on WordPad's **Quick Access Toolbar**.

h) Close WordPad and then close File Explorer.

3. Verify that your changes have automatically synchronized with OneDrive.

a) Using the **Switcher**, return to the OneDrive app.

 Note: Remember that you can access the **Switcher** by positioning your pointer in the top left corner of the screen and swiping down.

b) Place the pointer over the **Mental Fitness_revised** file to observe its tooltip.

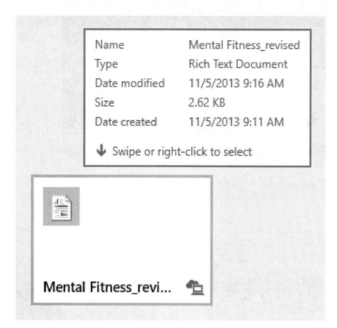

The **Date modified** value shows that the file was just edited.

c) Select the **Mental Fitness_revised** file to open it in WordPad.

d) Verify that your change to the date when the fitness program starts is reflected in your OneDrive documents.

4. Close WordPad.

5. Shut down the computer.

a) Open the **Settings Charm**.

b) Select the **Power** icon.

c) Select **Shut down** to close your account and turn off the computer.

Summary

In this lesson, you protected your PC against unauthorized access using alternative passwords, changed your privacy settings, and used Windows Defender to protect against viruses and spyware. You also used OneDrive to synchronize a file with the cloud. Using these methods, you'll be better prepared to protect against theft and have more flexibility when sharing, accessing, and backing up your data.

Why do you think Windows 8.1 gives password options such as a PIN and pictures? Do you think you might use a picture password at work? Why?

What might be the advantages of using OneDrive? How do you think you might use it in your job?

Note: Check your LogicalCHOICE Course screen for opportunities to interact with your classmates, peers, and the larger LogicalCHOICE online community about the topics covered in this course or other topics you are interested in. From the Course screen you can also access available resources for a more continuous learning experience.

Course Follow-Up

In this course, you used Windows 8.1 to learn about the power of personal computers and their usefulness to essentially everyone. You organized your files, customized your virtual workspace, and expanded your productivity. Now you'll be able to extend these valuable skills to both your work and home life, as complex tasks are made easier and more enjoyable with Windows 8.1.

What's Next?

You are encouraged to explore Windows 8.1 and related applications further. If you wish to learn more about word processing, spreadsheets, or other applications, Logical Operations has a full offering of courses for the beginning and advanced student. Some that might interest you include courses for Microsoft Office 2010 (including *Microsoft® Office Excel® 2010: Part 1*, *Microsoft® Office Word 2010: Part 1*, *Microsoft® Office PowerPoint® 2010: Part 1*, and *Microsoft® Office Outlook® 2010: Part 1*), as well as a full offering for Microsoft Office 2013 (including *Microsoft® Office Excel® 2013: Part 1*, *Microsoft® Office Word 2013: Part 1*, *Microsoft® Office PowerPoint® 2013: Part 1*, and *Microsoft® Office Outlook® 2013: Part 1*). Take whichever track suits the version of Office you work with the most.

You are also encouraged to explore Windows 8.1 further by actively participating in any of the social media forums set up by your instructor or training administrator through the **Social Media** tile on the LogicalCHOICE Course screen.

A | Other Windows 8.1 Features

Appendix Introduction

Microsoft® Windows® 8.1 allows multiple accounts on one PC, and you can add and delete users as needed. Windows 8.1 also offers a couple of ways of sharing, storing, and backing up your files. Along with OneDrive®, File History enables you to back up and restore your files, providing you with peace of mind.

TOPIC A

Create a New User Account

Windows 8.1 allows you to have more than one account on your PC, whether they are Microsoft Accounts or Local Accounts. Although you can use many of the apps and features of Windows 8.1 with a Local Account, accessing all that Windows 8.1 offers requires setting up a Microsoft Account.

Microsoft Account

With a Microsoft Account, you can download apps from the Windows Store, access online accounts such as OneDrive automatically, and sync multiple PCs so that they look and feel the same. If you have an Outlook® account or a Windows Live ID, you already have a Microsoft Account. You can use Windows 8.1 without a Microsoft Account by creating a Local Account, but you will be required to sign in when accessing some of the online features, and you will not be able to sync your computers.

Local Account

With a Local Account, you will still be able to use Desktop applications, go online, and use some of the Windows Store apps on your PC. You can also download applications from the Internet, or load them from a disk. However, you won't be able to use the Mail, Calendar, People, and OneDrive apps provided by Windows 8.1. Most of these, however, have equivalent programs that are available online. And, unlike with a Microsoft Account, you won't be able to sync, or automatically set up, other PCs to look and act like your primary PC, nor will you be able to download any apps from the Windows Store. If you set up your account as a Local Account, you can always change it to a Microsoft Account later.

 Access the Checklist tile on your LogicalCHOICE course screen for reference information and job aids on How to Create a Microsoft Account.

TOPIC B

File History

Once you have accumulated a number of files, or have files that are irreplaceable, backing up your data becomes very important. While the cloud is good for storing files you'd like to use on-the-go or with other computers, it can be quite expensive to store large quantities of data, and accidental deletions and changes can take place.

File History in Windows 8.1

It's always a good idea to have a backup, or a copy of your data kept in storage off of your PC, as insurance against accidental deletion, or in cases where your computer breaks or is lost. However, because most of us forget to make backups, or don't do it in a timely fashion, Windows 8.1 comes with File History, which automatically backs up your files. To ensure your files are safely stored off of your computer, File History requires you to use an external storage device or a network drive. Once File History is turned on and your storage device is designated, it will run in the background, saving the different versions of your files from your libraries, Desktop, contacts, and favorites automatically. If you use an external storage device, you must leave it attached to your PC for File History to automatically back up your files. If you choose to, you can specify folders to exclude from your backup, specify how often backups are created, or begin a manual backup. File History is available as part of the Windows 8.1 **PC settings** app as well as a traditional Desktop app. To restore a backed up version of a file, open File History from the Desktop and use the **Restore personal files** function.

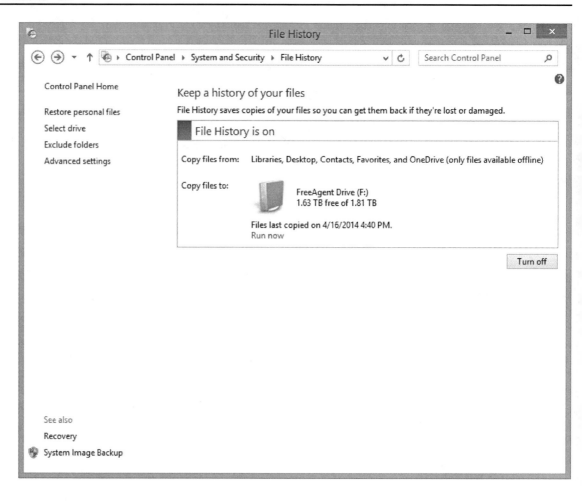

Save copies of your files automatically

Automatically back up copies of your personal files to another drive so you can get them back
if they're lost or damaged. File History backs up files in Documents, Music, Pictures, Videos and
Desktop, and the OneDrive files available offline on this PC.

File History
On

Back up your personal files on this PC to
FreeAgent Drive (F:), 1.63 TB free of 1.81 TB

Select a different drive

Your files were last backed up on 4/16/2014 4:40 PM.

Back up now

 **Access the Checklist tile on your LogicalCHOICE course screen for reference
information and job aids on How to Use File History.**

B | Help+Tips App

New to Windows 8.1 is the Help+Tips app, a Windows Store app created by Microsoft to assist new users in orienting themselves to the Windows 8.1 experience. This app can be used as a quick, helpful reference for users that may only be familiar with older versions of Windows or other operating systems like OS X and Linux. This app teaches the basics of navigation, app functionality, and computer settings in the Windows 8.1 environment. Additionally, if you have experience with the original Windows 8, you can see what's new and what's changed with the 8.1 upgrade.

Like all Windows Store apps, Help+Tips runs full screen and can be safely suspended in the background when you're not using it. Information is also presented in a large tile format for easy readability and navigation. Navigation command bars are similarly accessed by right-clicking within the app. As a default Windows Store app, Help+Tips comes with every installation of Windows 8.1 and has its tile pinned to the **Start** screen.

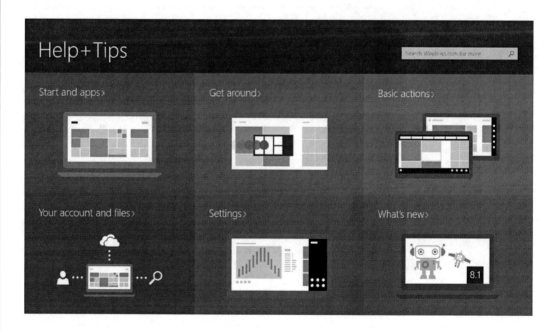

The following table describes the help topics in the Help+Tips app.

Help Topic	Teaches You
Start and apps	• What the **Start** screen is and how you can use it. • How to get more apps from the Windows Store. • How to see all of your apps. • How to access the Desktop.

Help Topic	Teaches You
Get around	• How to navigate to the **Start** screen. • How to use the **Switcher** to switch between apps. • How to see recently used apps. • How to close open apps.
Basic actions	• About the various Charms available. • How to open command bars in a Windows Store app. • How to use the snap feature to work with multiple apps side-by-side.
Your account and files	• About the advantages of using a Microsoft Account. • Where your files are saved, both locally and to OneDrive. • How to search for your files no matter where they are.
Settings	• How to change quick settings like brightness and volume. • How to shut down your computer. • How to access **PC settings**. • How to access app-specific settings.
What's new	• About the several new features, apps, and updates that come with Windows 8.1.

Windows.com Online Help

The Help+Tips app also includes the ability to search Microsoft's Windows.com website on the Internet for a much more in-depth look at all things Windows. When you enter a search term into the Help+Tips app's search bar, the Internet Explorer 11 Store app will open and snap to the right of the screen. If your search term is found within Windows.com's help database, you will be given a list of article links you may follow to learn more about a topic.

In addition, each help topic in Help+Tips has, at the far right of the screen, a **More on Windows.com** section. This section has several suggested links you can select to snap open Internet Explorer 11, taking you to the article on that topic.

C | Windows 8.1 Navigation Summary

The following tables summarize Windows 8.1 navigation tasks. Alternatives are shown for touch interface, mouse, and keyboard. Mouse button procedures refer to the default button layout. If you have configured your computer for a reverse button orientation, the buttons for these procedures will be the reverse of those shown here.

Moving Between Apps

Task	Touch Interface Procedure	Mouse Procedure	Keyboard Procedure
Cycle to the next app	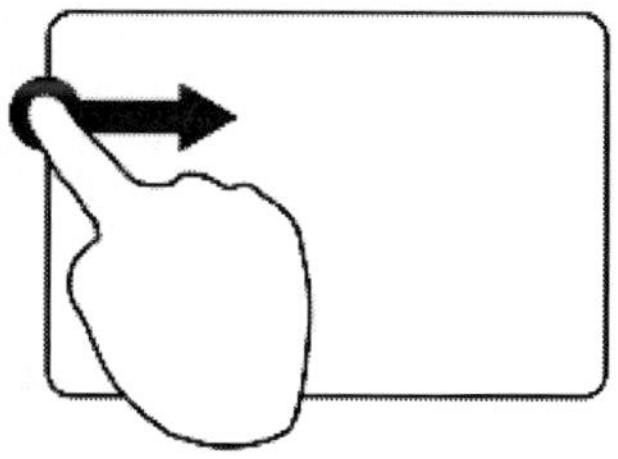 *Left edge swipe.* Press your finger on the left frame of the display screen (west of the screen area) and swipe your finger into the display area until the next app appears.	Position the mouse pointer in the upper-left corner of the display. When the app tile appears, left-click to cycle to the next app.	Press **Windows +Tab** until the app is selected.

Task	Touch Interface Procedure	Mouse Procedure	Keyboard Procedure
Show all previously used apps	*Left edge swipe in and out.* Press your finger on the left frame of the display screen (west of the screen area) and swipe your finger into the display area until the next app appears. Without lifting your finger, swipe back off-screen. Tap the app you want to return to.	Position the mouse pointer in the upper-left corner of the display. When the app tile appears, move the mouse pointer down the left edge until the other app tiles appear. Click an app tile to select it.	Press **Alt+Tab.** All applications are shown. While continuing to press **Alt,** press and release **Tab** until you have selected the application. Release **Alt** to switch to the selected application.
Cycle through classic Windows apps (those running within the Desktop app)	Tap the task bar icon to select the application.	Click the task bar icon to select the application.	Press **Alt+Tab** to cycle among applications running in Desktop.

Show Menus and Commands

Task	Touch Interface Procedure	Mouse Procedure	Keyboard Procedure
Show app commands	*Bottom edge swipe.* Press your finger on the bottom frame of the display screen (south of the display area) and swipe into the display area until the app commands appear. OR *Top edge swipe.* Press your finger on the top frame of the display screen (north of the screen area) and swipe your finger into the display area until the app commands appear.	Right-click a blank area of the app.	Press **Windows +Z.**
Hide app commands	*Bottom edge swipe* or *top edge swipe.* App commands are a toggle. The same gesture used to show the app commands also hide them.	Right-click a blank area of the app.	Press **Windows +Z.**

Task	Touch Interface Procedure	Mouse Procedure	Keyboard Procedure
Show the charms	*Right edge swipe.* Press your finger on the right frame of the display screen (east of the screen area) and swipe your finger into the display area until the charms appear.	Position the mouse pointer in the lower-right corner of the display.	Press **Windows +C** to toggle display of the charms.
Show Share	Show the charms and tap **Share.**	Show the charms and click **Share.**	Press **Windows +H** to show the settings for the current app.
Show Settings	Show the charms and tap **Settings.**	Show the charms and click **Settings.**	Press **Windows+I** to show the settings for the current app.
Show Search	Show the charms and tap **Search.**	Show the charms and click **Search.**	If you are at the **Start** screen, you can just start typing your search text and Search will automatically be displayed. Elsewhere, press **Windows+W** to open Search.

Window Layout

Task	Touch Interface Procedure	Mouse Procedure	Keyboard Procedure
Snap an app	*Left edge swipe in and partway out.* With an app already in the foreground, press your finger on the left frame of the display screen (west of the screen area) and swipe your finger into the display area until the next app appears. Pause until the snap bar appears, then release. The app snaps into place.	Position the mouse pointer in the upper-left corner of the display. When the app tile appears, move the mouse pointer down the left edge until the other app tiles appear. Drag an app tile slightly to the right until the snap pane appears. Release the mouse button to snap the app.	With two or more apps running, press **Windows+.** to toggle through snap layouts until the snap pane is open in the arrangement you want.
Unsnap an app	Drag the snap border off screen.	Drag the snap border off screen.	Press **Windows +Right arrow** to toggle through snap layouts until the snap pane is closed.
Move Snap bar	Tap and drag the Snap bar to the other side of the display.	Drag the Snap bar to the other side of the display.	

Other Tasks

Task	Touch Interface Procedure	Mouse Procedure	Keyboard Procedure
Click a button	*Tap* on the button with your finger.	Position the mouse pointer over the button and press the left button.	Press tab until to the button or link is selected, then press **Enter**.
Close an app	*Top edge swipe to the bottom edge.* Press your finger on the top frame of the display screen (north of the screen area) and swipe your finger into the display area and keep going until you finger exits the bottom of the display. The app you swiped over will be closed.	Drag from just below the top of edge of the display off the bottom edge of the display. You can also position the mouse at the top of the page until the title bar is displayed, then select the **Close** button.	Press **Alt+F4**.
Scroll the display left, right, up, or down	*Swipe.* Press your finger in the display area and drag your finger in the direction you want to scroll the display.	• Use the mouse to click the scroll bars. • Spin the mouse-wheel to scroll a list.	Press the left, right, up, or down-arrow key to scroll in that direction.

Task	Touch Interface Procedure	Mouse Procedure	Keyboard Procedure
Select a tile or icon	Tap and hold briefly; then swipe down about 1/4" until the check mark appears.	Right-click the tile.	Press **Tab** until one of the tiles is selected. Press arrow keys to select the tile you want. Press **Spacebar** to select the tile.
Toggle display orientation lock	Press the rotation lock button.		Press **Windows +O** to cycle through display orientation settings.
Shift screen display to a projector or second monitor	Show the charms and tap **Devices**. Tap **Project**. Tap the display option.	Show the charms and select **Devices**. Select **Project**. Select the display option.	Press **Windows +P**. Press an arrow key to select the display option, then press **Enter**.
Peek at the Desktop	*Not applicable*		Press **Windows+,** to peek at the Desktop app. Release the **Windows** key to return to what you were viewing before.
Move app to a different monitor	*Not applicable*		• Press **Windows +PgUp** to move the **Start** screen or app to the monitor on the left. • Press **Windows +PgDn** to move the **Start** screen or app to the monitor on the right.

Task	Touch Interface Procedure	Mouse Procedure	Keyboard Procedure
Capture a screen shot	*Not applicable*		Press **Windows +Print Screen** to capture a screen shot to your Pictures/ Screenshots directory.
Lock the device	Press the power button.		Press **Window +L**.

Lesson Labs

Lesson labs are provided for certain lessons as additional learning resources for this course. Lesson labs are developed for selected lessons within a course in cases when they seem most instructionally useful as well as technically feasible. In general, labs are supplemental, optional unguided practice and may or may not be performed as part of the classroom activities. Your instructor will consider setup requirements, classroom timing, and instructional needs to determine which labs are appropriate for you to perform, and at what point during the class. If you do not perform the labs in class, your instructor can tell you if you can perform them independently as self-study, and if there are any special setup requirements.

Lesson Lab 1-1
Managing Tiles and the Start Screen

Activity Time: 15 minutes

Scenario

Your company just made the switch from Windows 7 to Windows 8.1. Your IT department has migrated all your contacts and files, and as many settings as possible to the new setup. You have reviewed all of your files and are satisfied that you have everything you need. However, you want to set up your Windows 8.1 environment to accommodate your typical work flow. So, you decide to rearrange the tiles on the **Start** screen, pin your commonly used applications to the **Start** screen, and personalize your background and account picture.

---

1. Move the following Store apps to a new, middle column on the **Start** screen: Photos, Camera, and Store.

2. From the **Apps View** screen, pin the following Store apps to the **Start** screen: Reader, Scan, and Calculator.

3. Make a small tile larger, and a large tile smaller.

4. Use the semantic zoom feature to move the group of Reader, Scan, and Calculator to the left of the entertainment column you created in the first step.

5. Add or change your account picture. You can use any image stored on the PC.

6. Return to the **Start** screen.

Lesson Lab 2-1
Navigating Multiple Windows Store Apps

Activity Time: 15 minutes

Scenario

You're a salesperson for a hardware manufacturer based in Rochester, New York. One of your job duties is traveling across the country to demonstrate the company's products to prospective clients. You have a new lead: a furniture company located in Harrisburg, Pennsylvania. You'll need directions to get down there, and before you begin the trip next week, you remember hearing talk of a major storm hitting the Northeast sometime soon. You decide to confirm these reports while simultaneously plotting a course south to Harrisburg. You'll also want to check the weather in any towns and cities along the way, just to be sure.

1. Launch the Maps app.

2. Use the command bar to look up directions:
   a) **From**: Your current location.
   b) **To**: 100 Wildwood Way, Harrisburg, PA

3. Snap the Maps app to a side.

4. Open the Weather app so that it snaps to the other side.

5. Adjust the Maps app so that it takes up more of the screen and zooms in on the directions.

6. Look up Harrisburg, PA in the Weather app and take note of any severe weather occurring the following Monday.

7. Look up the weather for more cities your route takes you through.

8. Return to the **Start** screen when you're finished.

Lesson Lab 3-1
Managing Files and Libraries

Activity Time: 15 minutes

Data Files

C:\091128Data\Working with Desktop Applications\palm trees.JPG

C:\091128Data\Working with Desktop Applications\rio.JPG

C:\091128Data\Working with Desktop Applications\swiss alps.JPG

Scenario

You are a photographer who specializes in location photography for travel publications, international businesses, and marketing firms. You recently switched to Windows 8.1 and are excited about the addition of the ribbon to File Explorer. You have been storing your files in a folder at the root level of your hard drive, but feel it will be easier to manage the large number of image files you regularly work with by placing them within a folder in your local **Documents** folder. You decide to create a folder there, and then to begin the process of moving your image files to the new folder.

---

1. In File Explorer, navigate to your local **Documents** folder, and then create a folder named *images*.

2. Using the File Explorer ribbon, copy and paste the **C:\091128Data\Working with Desktop Applications\palm trees.JPG** file to the new **images** folder.

3. Using the File Explorer ribbon, move the **rio.JPG** and **swiss alps.JPG** files to the **images** folder.

4. Verify the images display in the **images** folder.

5. Close File Explorer.

Lesson Lab 4-1
Using Internet Explorer 11

Activity Time: 15 minutes

Scenario

You are a television reporter for a local station in a relatively large metropolitan area. As such, you often cover news stories that deal with local, national, and international events. Your station just started using Windows 8.1, mainly to accommodate new mobile devices for reporters and video journalists. You want to get your desktop PC set up with all of the tools you are used to using on a daily basis. One of your top priorities is creating links to many of the news sites you use to research regional, national, and international news. You decide to save the links as tiles to the **Start** screen for quick access.

---

1. Launch the Internet Explorer 11 Windows Store app.

2. Navigate to **reuters.com** and pin the website to the **Start** screen.

3. Use **Internet Explorer** to search for and pin a second website of your choosing to the **Start** screen.

4. Pin another site of your choosing to the **Start** screen, and then add it to your favorites.

5. Switch to the Desktop version of Internet Explorer, and then verify that the website you added to your **Favorites** appears in the **Favorites** toolbar.

6. Close both the Desktop and the Windows Store versions of Internet Explorer 11.

7. If necessary, navigate to the **Start** screen and verify the links work from the newly added tiles, and then close Internet Explorer 11.

Lesson Lab 6–1
Using Windows 8.1 Security Features

Activity Time: 15 minutes

Data Files

C:\091128Data\Using Windows 8.1 Security Features\food.jpg

Scenario

You are the General Manager of one location for a casual dining restaurant chain. You have received an email from the IT department indicating a number of company computers have been infected with a virus, and the situation may have been initiated by an employee of the company. The IT department has directed you to run a virus scan using Windows Defender and switch to using a 4-digit PIN or a picture password until they can determine which password was compromised and perform a password reset.

---

1. Run a **Quick** scan using Windows Defender.

2. Set a 4-digit PIN.

3. Record your 4-digit PIN:

   PIN: _____

4. Verify the 4-digit PIN has been set by signing out and then signing back in using the 4-digit PIN.

5. Set a picture password using the **C:\091128Data\Using Windows 8.1 Security Features \food.jpg** image.

6. Record your three gestures here:

   Gestures: _____

7. Verify the picture password has been set by signing out and then signing back in using the picture password.

Solutions

ACTIVITY 1-1: Identifying Personal Computer Components and Applications

1. How are desktop PCs, laptops, and tablets similar?

   A: Answers may include: They all have hardware, software, and operating systems; they all have input, processing, and output devices; and they all accomplish similar tasks.

2. How are desktop PCs, laptops, and tablets different?

   A: Answers may include: the size of units; portability; laptops and tablets have input, processing, and output in one unit, whereas a desktop is made up of separate devices. Some use a mouse and keyboard, whereas others use touch screens.

3. What is the purpose of the operating system?
   - ○ To create spreadsheets
   - ◉ To create a work environment for application software
   - ○ To process data from a database
   - ○ To share data in documents

   Although database software is specifically designed to manage large quantities of data, consider accepting spreadsheets as a possible answer.

4. Which type of software would be best for gathering and sorting through the large amount of data contained in the surveys?
   - ○ Spreadsheet
   - ○ Word processor
   - ◉ Database
   - ○ Presentation

5. If you want to type up a report and create a slide show, which two types of software would you likely use?
   - ☐ Spreadsheet
   - ☑ Word processor
   - ☐ Database
   - ☑ Presentation

6. **What types of applications might you use for your daily work?**

   A: Answers will vary depending on the user's needs, but may include word processor, spreadsheet, database, presentation, project management, educational, business, or industrial applications.

Glossary

add-on
Also called a plugin, this adds new functionality to a web browser, such as video player software.

application
Commonly shortened to "app," this is software that can perform a wide range of tasks for the user.

body
The portion of the window where work is displayed. The body of directory windows include the **Navigation** pane and **Content** pane.

boot
When the PC is turned on, the process of self-tests it performs before loading the operating system.

Charms
Context-sensitive tools available from everywhere in Windows 8.1 that provide access to system-wide functions.

Clipboard
The Windows feature that stores cut or copied text or images and enables them to be pasted or moved within a document or to another application.

cloud computing
The use of software and hardware resources that are delivered as a service over the Internet.

context menu
A menu displayed when right-clicking icons, the taskbar, and the Desktop that provides quick access to common tasks. Also called jump lists.

contextual tab
Additional tabs that appear on the ribbon when you work with certain objects or functions.

Desktop
A Windows 8.1 app that provides an environment for running classic Windows software applications, as well as performing system functions like file management, Control Panel access, Windows Defender, File History, and so forth.

Desktop application
A software application designed to run in a traditional window on the Desktop.

Desktop icon
A small labeled picture on the Desktop that acts as a shortcut for running a program or opening a file.

drag
Move your pointer over an item on your screen, and press and hold the left mouse button as you move the mouse. Release the button when the item has been moved to the desired location.

File Explorer
The Windows 8.1 component used to view and manage the computer's filing system.

folder
A directory used to store files.

hardware
The physical components of a computer, including input devices like a mouse and keyboard; output devices like a printer and monitor; and internal components like a processor and hard drive.

Internet portal
A website that gathers information from many sources to present it on a single site.

keyboard shortcut
Keys or key combinations used to execute a menu command.

library
A directory similar to a folder that does not store files but instead tracks where files and folders are located and presents them in a single area.

live tiles
A tile that displays real-time information, even when the app is not running.

Notification area
The right side of the taskbar that displays icons for system functions and shows messages about computer issues.

OneDrive
The Microsoft cloud-computing solution bundled with Windows 8.1. It enables users to store and access files from any equipped computer.

OS
(operating system) The software environment on top of which apps are able to run. Operating systems manage the physical hardware of a computer.

reboot
The process of turning the PC off and back on to apply any updates and perform clean-up procedures.

Recycle Bin
The directory that stores deleted folders and files. Folders and files can be restored to their original locations until the Recycle Bin is emptied.

restore point
A user-specified healthy computer state that can be returned to in the event that the computer becomes infected with malicious software.

ribbon
The interface element that includes tabs and commands for managing, editing, and viewing files.

screen saver
A feature that displays a blank screen or series of pictures after a period of computer inactivity.

search engine
Software, usually on a website, that searches the World Wide Web based on the terms you entered into it. The search engine returns a list of websites that are most relevant to the terms you entered.

Snap
A feature to show up to four apps on the same screen at once, or eight spread across two high-resolution monitors. Lower-resolution monitors are only able to display two snapped apps at once.

snap bar
The dividing line between snapped apps that can be dragged to change the size of the apps.

software
A set of instructions that enables your computer to perform specific tasks. Contrast with hardware.

Switcher
An interface element used to flip between open apps.

taskbar
The Desktop element along the bottom of the screen that displays icons for open or pinned apps.

tile
A graphic box, containing text and/or graphics, that represents a Windows 8.1 app and provides a means of opening the app it represents. Some tiles can also show preview information about the app in "live tile" mode.

toolbar
An interface element of Desktop apps like Internet Explorer that add menus and controls to the app window.

tooltip
A hint that displays the name or function of a tile, icon, or menu option when you hover your pointer over the item.

URL
(Uniform Resource Locator) The unique address for a website on the Internet.

web browser
A program that locates and displays information on the World Wide Web.

Windows Defender
A built-in program that protects Windows computers from malicious software and unwanted downloads.

Windows Store app
A software application designed to run in the new application environment introduced with Windows 8.

Index

A

Account ID menu *18*
add-on *99*
app command bar *15*
apps
  Close App function *35*
  Desktop applications *13*
  multiple-app functionality *34*
  types of *3*
  Windows Store apps *13, 29*

B

Bing
  POPULAR NOW pane *81*
  preferences *90*
body of the window *62*
booting *7*

C

Charms
  Settings Charm *112*
  Share Charm *91, 143*
  Start screen *24*
Clipboard *69*
cloud *143*
cloud computing *143*
Context menus *45*
contextual tabs *53*

D

Desktop
  background *121*
  icons *47*

  Personalization window *121*
Desktop windows
  elements of *60*
  managing *63*
dialog boxes *46*
documents
  create new *68*
  open existing *68*
  save *68*

E

Ease of Access menu
  features *9*

F

File Explorer *51*
folders *51*
Frequent menu *88, 89*

H

hardware components *2*

I

Internet Explorer 11
  command bar *87*
  Search bar *87*
  Tabs menu *89*
  toolbars *100*
  using search suggestions *87*
  window elements *100*
internet portal *80*

K

keyboard shortcuts *45*

L

libraries *51*
Lock screen *7*

M

mouse properties *122*

N

Notification area *45*

O

OneDrive
    Share Charm *143*
operating system, *See* OS
OS *3*

P

passwords
    picture *11, 131*
    PIN *11, 130*
    requirements *10*
PC settings menu *113*
plugin, *See* add-on
pointers *122*
Print *69*
privacy menu *135*

Q

Quick Access Toolbar *61*

R

reboot *7*
Recycle Bin *53*
Redo *69*
restore point *139*
ribbon *53*

S

screen savers *122*
scroll bar *16*
search categories menu *81*
search engines
    examples of *80*

Shut Down menu *10*
Sign In screen *8*
Snap feature
    Snap bar *36*
Start button *15*
Start screen *13*
Switcher *34*

T

taskbar *44*
tile groups *110*
tiles
    dragging *14*
    live tiles *14*
tooltips *14, 45*

U

Undo *69*
Uniform Resource Locator, *See* URL
URL *81*

W

web browsers
    examples of *80*
Windows Defender
    Real-time protection *139*